A KETLEY MON

Terry Lowe

A Ketley Mon

Terry Lowe is a native of Ketley and was educated at the Ketley Junior and Senior Schools followed by further education at the Walker Technical College at Hartshill, Oakengates.

In 1964 he completed a 6-year Indentured apprenticeship as a maintenance fitter at Joseph Sankey and Sons at their Castle Works in Hadley. Terry joined the Shropshire Constabulary in 1967 and served as a constable at Wellington, Market Drayton, Woore and Oakengates. He was appointed the first Drugs Liaison Officer for the Wellington Division in 1974 and was promoted as a Sergeant Instructor at the West Mercia Headquarters, Worcester in 1978.

Following spells as a detective Sergeant on C I D at Evesham and Droitwich he returned to his home County for the final 14 years of his service where he pioneered local police and Community relations as the Press Liaison Officer for Telford Police. As the police spokesman for the area he became known as 'the voice of the Police' throughout the county through the medium of television, radio and press involvement.

He retired at 53 in 1996 to concentrate on his writing. A married man with 3 grown-up children, and 6 grandchildren, he lives in Wellington, Shropshire. Terry is well known locally as a 'film buff' and a life-long supporter of Manchester United Football Club. He has a passion for the music and poetry of American singer/composer, Bob Dylan.

Acknowledgments:

Shropshire records and Research Centre, Coalport Museum Library, Shropshire Star newspaper, Telford Journal/Wellington Journal and Shrewsbury News, Shrewsbury Chronicle, Eddowes Journal, A Victorian History of Great Britain, C. Hadfield (The canals of the West Midlands), Ivor J Brown (Shropshire Tragedies, A collection of old ballads), C B Mercer (The Cinderloo Affair), W Howard Williams (East Shropshire Canals) The American Dictionary of Who's Who.

I am also indebted to the following people:

Paul Luter (Researcher), Trevor Williams, Alan Harper, Len and Graham Corbett, John Hassell, Mary Jones, Mrs D A Jones, Dianne Warner, The Upton Family, Alf Thompson, Ray Phillips, John Whittingham, Mary France, Trisha Gentleman, Amy Parry, Tom Chappell, Ken Jones, Alan Parton, Ernie Dabbs for being so persistent, Suzanne Overton for Proof Reading.

Terry Lowe/British Bus Publishing

Published by British Bus Publishing Ltd, 16 St Margaret's Drive, Wellington, Telford, TF1 3PH, January 2000

ISBN 1 897990 99 5

LIST OF CHAPTERS

Front cover: **The Ketley Offices being demolished in 1936-37.** *(courtesy of the Shropshire Star)*
Frontispiece: **1895 picture of the Lewis family and friends pictured outside their home in the Dingle.**
Rear Cover: **The author as a young boy.**

BRUCE GROCOTT MP
Telford Constituency

HOUSE OF COMMONS
LONDON SW1A 0AA

FOREWORD

BRUCE GROCOTT MP

This is a book by a Ketley man and the love of the place where Terry Lowe was born and bred shines through every page. It is a book that Terry says he felt he had to write and I for one am glad that he did.

He is especially strong in his descriptions of the difficulties of life for the majority of people of Ketley, particularly at the time of the Industrial Revolution and through the Victorian era. There are vivid passages dealing with the life of the miners, the absence of safety precautions, the low pay and poor working conditions.

The book describes Ketley in all its moods – Ketley at war, Ketley at play, the schools and the churches. Not surprisingly from an author who has spent his working life in the police, there are dramatic descriptions of the more notorious crimes in Ketley's history.

The whole of the Wrekin area has an extraordinarily rich and varied history. Terry Lowe's book, his labour of love, ensures that Ketley's role is properly and affectionately recorded.

London (0171) 219 5058   Telford (01952) 507747

This Book is dedicated to my Grandchildren

Peter Zach Overton
Rebecca Louise Lowe
Ryan Luke Evans
Thomas Reic Lowe
David Mark Overton
Sean Anthony Evans

INTRODUCTION

For those of you who are familiar with the area of Telford known as Ketley I imagine the immediate question on your lips will be, why bother to write a book about it? Or perhaps if you haven't heard of it then you may be asking yourself where or what on earth IS Ketley? The answer to the second question is merely a matter of geological fact. Present day Ketley occupies approximately one and a quarter square miles in the new town of Telford, Shropshire. Telford became a Unitary Authority in 1998 and severed the traditional ties with county of Shropshire. The great Roman road of Watling Street sub-divides the town that sprang up on its route. In turn the road became Ketley's creator, saviour and downfall in various periods over the last 2,000 years.

The answer to the first question has a slightly simpler explanation. There has never been, as far as I am aware, a book written about the history, heritage and people of the Ketley area. As a passionately proud native of Ketley (known locally as 'Ketley-ites) I was, naturally, aware of its role in the Industrial Revolution and the resolute grit and toughness of its inhabitants, but I knew little of the parochial history of the town.

When I retired from the local police force in 1996 two events steered me in the direction of a long-promised task to research my family tree. Sadly my father had passed away that year and in the way that nature often balances the books, a new grandson was born into the Lowe family. Thomas Eric Lowe was the first of my six grandchildren to be born a name carrier and as a bonus he lives in my beloved Ketley.

I inherited my pride for my hometown from my father and grand-parents who instilled in me a sense of heritage and the importance of family values.

In the autumn of 1964 a family photograph of four generations of male Lowes, my grandfather Bert and father Len with myself and my two-month-old son Russell captured a combined age of 144 years.

Thirty-two years later, on the occasion of my retirement, a similar picture with my dad and myself framing Russell with his new son Thomas, covered a combined age range of 162 years, completing a rare double.

My hope is that in another thirty years or so a unique treble of generation's photographs may hang in some future Lowe household.

Family research is obsessive. I see it as a journey, not a conventional trip by wheel, hoof or foot but more akin to a surreal trip back down the mists of time. It becomes an all-consuming passion. You find one piece of the hereditary jigsaw and you thirst for more! The skills I had gathered in the police force equipped me perfectly for the task ahead. Patiently

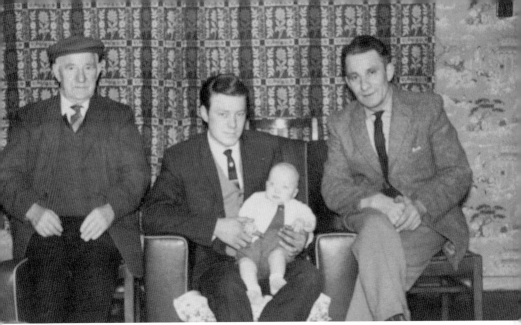

Four Generations of the Lowe family taken in 1964. *(Terry Lowe)*

perusing documents and directories, following clues and gathering evidence and facts to establish the linear links reproduced the feeling of being back at work.

The whole area of family research is now a growth industry. There appears to be a healthy compulsive desire for everybody to trace his or her roots. During my quest I began to notice the same familiar faces at the local research centre and records office, each with that look of 'anticipation', as if they were about to find THE piece to fit into THEIR ancestral jigsaw! Rows of researchers staring Zombie-like into microfilm and microfiche machines was a normal sight.

The induced silence in the room was broken only by an excited 'YES' uttered as another reader discovers a new relative. I enjoyed immensely the experience of research and the gathering of information from census and official registries.

The satisfaction gained during my months of researching provided the thrill that had disappeared from my life with the advent of retirement from the police. Finally, following many months and long days at research centres, churches graveyards, and records offices I was able to chart twelve generations of Lowes from 1694 to the present. The realisation that my ancestors had lived through the reigns of thirteen monarchs from William and Mary to our present Queen and, more importantly through some of the most significant events in this country's history provided the inspiration to find out more about their lifestyles and background.

Four generations of the Lowe family one generation on. This picture from 1996 shows. *(Terry Lowe)*

Try to imagine my joy upon the discovery of a Lowe-Ketley connection which had commenced in 1792 when my great, great, great grandfather, James Lowe was born and christened in Beveley, Ketley.

I can only say that I was as proud as a peacock at the revelation that every male in my tree up to and including my new grandson had been born within the area known as Ketley. Inspiration gradually merged into obsession.

For me the downside of my months of effort came with the lack of detail concerning my earlier ancestors. I was left wanting to know more. What was their quality of life? What were their hopes and aspirations? I was determined to probe deeper into the Ketley connection.

Oh how I wished now that I'd questioned my parents and grandparents for more information about their respective close relatives. That missed opportunity would haunt me in the coming months. A great frustration came with that lack of detail. I yearned to know more. I accepted that I would never have a physical image and that I could only picture my newly found relatives in my mind's eye. My ancestors had lived and worked in the heart of the local Industrial Revolution and I knew nothing of their contribution or lifestyle, other than the basic fact that they were miners and iron men. For example, my great grandfather Felix Lowe died in 1933 but I only have a sketchy idea of what he looked like. There are no photographs of the old ironworker and the only description that exists is of a silver-haired old man who smoked a clay pipe, liked his daily pint in the 'Horse Shoes' pub (later re-named Horseshoes) and spent his final days tending his allotment. This was a man who was born in the early 1850s and died just ten years before I was born.

In retrospect I realise that the chronicling of my family tree was the period when the fuse was lit for me to write the story of my town.

I can pinpoint precisely when the concept of a book about Ketley first entered my brain. It was when Anna Sydenham, head teacher at my old school approached me to attend the centenary celebration at Ketley School. She had invited me to say a few words on behalf of the present and former pupils.

I considered it a great honour and concentrated my mind on the theme of my address. It suddenly dawned on me that I would be representing generations of Ketley school pupils past and present, including the very ancestors I had recently discovered and two grandchildren who currently attend the school!

This realisation heightened my sense of the historic importance of the occasion and the need to pay proper respect to the hundreds of Ketley kids who had attended the school.

On the night my brief was to speak for about fifteen minutes in what was a tight schedule. (Many would say a veritable impossibility for me, I believe that members of the audience were taking bets on how long I would run overtime.)

As I rose to speak I became aware that the esteemed audience contained a fair number of people for whom I have deep respect, including former teachers and personal friends. That fact produced a moment of blind panic. The sudden adrenaline rush inspired me to deliver my address in the form of a homage to the former and present pupils of the school into which I wove details of my recently completed family tree with a strong emphasis on my Ketley connection.

For once in my life (to the disappointment of many that had wagered against it) I finished my piece near enough on time.

A few months later I received a telephone call which went something like this; "You've got to write a book about Ketley!" "Who is this?" "Ernie Dabbs, you may not remember me but I was at the Ketley school celebration when you spoke about your family links with the school, you MUST write this book."

My first thoughts were 'who is this madman and how did he get my unlisted number?' Making a mental note to speak to the head teacher about giving my telephone number to all and sundry, I politely dismissed him with a promise to think about his proposition. The truth is I had no intention of ringing him back. My mind was on an upcoming trip to a wedding of a friend's daughter in America so I promptly forgot all about Mr

Dabbs and proceeded to get on with my life. Fortunately for me the persistent Mr Dabbs called again and insisted that we meet for a chat. I was about to say I was unavailable when he spoke the magic words; "Let me buy you a pint at the White Lion."

The smouldering fuse, which had been lit a year before suddenly fanned into life when Ernie showed me some old photographs of Ketley. The images of my boyhood Ketley stirred long-forgotten memories and I could feel myself nibbling at the bait.

Now in his mid sixties, Ernie is, like me, another proud Ketley man, from the 'Poplars' area of Ketley a little haven that nestles in an area about 200 yards north of the White Lion public house. His memories and recollections pre-date my own by ten years but, as often happens when two like-minded enthusiasts get together we chatted like a couple of excited schoolboys as one memory would 'spark off' another memory in the other person. I was now hooked.

My only experience of writing apart from school essays and police reports was a series of anecdotal articles written for the local Shropshire Star newspaper during my last year as Telford's police-press liaison officer. During this period I had often wondered if I could write a 'proper book'. A close friend once told me that everybody has at least one book inside them and I convinced myself that mine would to be the story of my birthplace. Journalist friends had been prompting me to write my memoirs for years. The truth is, I was in awe of the task and I knew that I would spend endless sleepless nights for the rest of my life if I didn't have a go at it.

I found myself returning to the by now familiar arena of research and hours of back-bending work studying dusty old newspapers, maps and documents.

During the next few months I began to warm to the task as a wealth of facts and material emerged, not only from the written word but also the spoken evidence of the people of Ketley who I had sought out for their memories and stories.

The grapevine ensured that very soon everybody seemed to know of my quest. Ketley people stopped me in the street or rang me up with information. I began to collect an impressive range of material and rare unpublished photographs.

I was particularly thrilled at the discovery of fascinating stories and the colourful characters that have enriched the history of the Ketley area.

As I probed deeper and deeper into Ketley's history I began to realise how important a role it had played, especially in the early days of the Industrial Revolution of the 18th Century. The rich vein of characters and incidents finally convinced me that I HAD to write this book. By this time I was well and truly hooked and this is the result.

KETLEY'S EARLY HISTORY

The boundaries of Ketley have changed little since the 18th Century and the present-day territory is clearly defined. Travellers from the east pass by the town of Oakengates to the left of them as Watling Street, which is also known as the A5 road, carries them to the borders of Ketley, which commence at the Hartshill roundabout. This stretch now forms part of the A518 but will always be known as the A5, Roman Road.

A Peugeot car dealer and garage marks the spot together with an official sign, a rare marker celebrating Ketley's existence! Continuing east and just over a mile later the boundary ends at Bennetts Bank, the site of the old Youth Club. The Shrewsbury to Birmingham railway line is its northern border and the Ketley Brook slip road to the M54 motorway at the Wrekin Retail Park sweeps south to the Rock Bank and its southern borderline. With the market towns of Wellington, Hadley, Oakengates and Dawley ringing it, the Ketley hamlets of Mossey Green, Overdale, Red Lake, and Beveley nestle within its borders.

Fascinated by the origin of place names I decided to begin my story on what I considered a logical basis by tracking down the evolution of the name Ketley.

I discovered that the name has various explanations but is believed to be of Anglo Saxon origin. Literally translated it means, 'Wood of the Wild Cat'. The 'ley' part indicates that it was an area from which a vast forest had originally covered the whole district and had now been cleared away.

The 'Ket' part is describes in Bocock's book on Shropshire place names as 'Cytel': for example, as Malinslee was the lee of Malin so Ketley was the lee of Cytel forming 'Cytelslee'.

The Oxford dictionary of place names defines it as the more colourful Anglo Saxon name of 'Wildcat Wood'. During the Saxon times long-since extinct animals including the indigenous large wildcats freely roamed the countryside hunting and waging war against their primary enemy, man. So with a little imagination it is easy to see how the Old Saxon name came about.

The Victorian County History of Shropshire confirms much of the name origin when it describes two thirds of the area as predominantly wooded.

Within the boundary of 'Lee Gomery Manor', in 1086 the Ketley part accounted for a large portion of the two leagues of woodland within the eastern and southern parts of the Manor. Presumably Ketley is not mentioned in the Doomsday Book because of its attachment to Lee Gomery at that time. The earliest significant mention of Ketley can be found in 1269 when the ancient parish of Wombridge contained that part of early Ketley that was then known as 'Ketley Wood'. It covered the area that we now call Red Lake and swept eastwards down to the present day area of Ketley Town. A tiny glimpse of the population of Ketley during medieval times is revealed in the tax roll of 1269.

A total of fourteen taxpayers are listed in the area, which was still being referred to by its Saxon name of 'Cytel's Lea'.

On the Shropshire Land Subsidy Roll of 1327 Ketley is referred to as 'Ketteleye', the earliest reference I could find to the present-day title. The Roll provides an intriguing list of medieval tenants! The Norman influence is prominent in the strangely named, 'Joh'e le Gaterherd', and 'Matill Bonde'. There is an obvious reference to the famous local Wrekin hill sited at the foot of the Ercall on the outskirts of nearby Wellington within the name of another roll subject who rejoiced in the title of 'Rog de le Wrekene'.

Little is recorded of Ketley's role in the Roman occupation in 46 BC and even less before that, when the indigenous peoples were plagued by the ancient seafarers called Phoenicians. Unlike the Phoenicians who raped and pillaged the land the Romans brought a civilised culture to the islands in the shape of their spa baths and great roads. Watling Street was the great Roman road stretching from London to Holyhead on the Welsh coast. Upon that near 200-mile route many Roman stations were established including Uxacona and the fourth largest Roman city in Britain which was known as Uriconium. These Stations are known today as Oakengates and Wroxeter respectively. The Roman Empire's rule ended in the 5th Century when Rome was in turn invaded by the Goths and our island was left to the ravages of various raiders.

Teutonic pirates in their long black ships, Viking hoards, Danish Angles, Saxons and Jutes eventually drove the original Celtic stock into the mountains where they survived and evolved. Except in these areas, Christianity and the Celtic language had died out, and Britain, as it was called then, came to be known as Angle Land, after the Angles. A marriage between the Anglo-Saxon and Celtic languages, and later the Norman, evolved the English we speak today. The new Angles divided the country into small Kingdoms; the Midlands and parts of Wales became Mercia.

Commodities such as quarry stone and coal has existed in this land since time began and the Romans had used them for building homes and defences as well as fuelling forges to make weapons, utensils and transport.

It was in the 13th Century that Thomas Tuschet, the then Lord of Leegomery Manor, granted perpetual quarrying and coal mining rights to the monks of Wombridge Priory who needed the Ketley stone for repairs to their buildings.

In exchange the monks made an agreement to pray for the souls of Thomas and his wife Marjory every St. Valentines Day, perpetuating the Tuschet name.

In the early 17th Century, such was the volume of coal mined locally, one of the areas in Ketley gained the name of 'Coal Pit Bank'. This was later to change to the more familiar name of Ketley Bank. A sandstone quarry was referred to as being 'active' in the Ketley area and there was mention of coal and ironstone being taken near to the ground's surface in the late 16th Century. The early industrial reputation of the area was gradually evolving to its date with destiny and the industrial revolution of the 18th Century.

During the early 17th Century miners cottages are recorded on the Ketley stretch of Watling Street and it was evident that an increasing number of families were living entirely off an early coal mining industry.

A hearth or chimney tax was introduced in 1662 and the proclamation stated that every fire, hearth or stove in every dwelling would be subject to a two shilling (10p) tax. This money was made payable in England and Wales at Michaelmas – the festival of St Michael held on the 29th of September each year – to 'the King and all His Heirs'. As with all taxes the populace hated it. Fortunately some of those in power also disliked it, declaring it 'an abomination and criminal' so it was eventually replaced with a window tax.

A mere twelve persons were recorded in the list for 1672. The Ketley and Ketley Wood residents included names that are familiar around the area today. William Podmore, John Groom and Peter Phillips are just three examples of the local names that remain today.

Just over ten years later there was a report that residents of Coal Pit Bank were complaining that extreme poverty was forcing them to send their wives and small children to work in the crude coal pits. This provides an insight into the rapid growth and general development of the area.

From 1715 Lord Gower leased all the coal, ironstone and limestone to Richard Hartshorne, master collier of Ketley. The pits, which were rich in coal and ironstone were mostly in the Ketley Wood and Coal Pit Bank areas and enabled Hartshorne to become the leading mining entrepreneur of his day. Born around 1654 in nearby Malinslee, Richard became extremely rich and successful and, in 1721, he began the building of a family home at Coal Pit Bank. This fine structure survives today as 'Bank House', Ketley Bank. Without a doubt Richard Hartshorne, who died in December 1733, at the grand old age of seventy-nine, laid the foundation of the coal industry in the Ketley area.

With local ironstone, being sent to an early Coalbrookdale furnace, and the area, known now as Ketley Sands supplying exclusively the sand for the nearby Horsehay ironworks, the rumblings of the Industrial Revolution were being witnessed. The name Ketley was becoming almost synonymous with the new industry. The 18th Century literally forged and shaped the New Britain. English merchants were leaders in developing commerce, which in turn increased the demand for more goods.

There was also a growing interest in scientific investigation and invention, stimulating the movement and advancing ideas at an astonishing rate.

The first users of the new steam engines were the coal and iron industries who were destined to become the leading industries in the new-age of machinery.

As early as 1720 dozens of steam engines were in operation, including several in Ketley. Their primary use was to pump out the water, which usually flooded the deep shafts of the coal mines.

In the furnaces they were vital, being used to pump water to help create the draught. Iron was becoming scarce and costly and production was falling off because England's forests could not supply enough charcoal for smelting the ore. The early ironmasters like Hartshorne had, for years, been experimenting with coal as a fuel for smelting when finally the Darby family after three generations of effort, succeeded with coal which had been transformed into coke. This created an increased and renewed demand for coal. The foundations for the British coal industry, which had been laid some forty years earlier, cemented Ketley's immediate future.

The next groundbreaking step was taken in the 1780s when Henry Cort developed the process of puddling and rolling. The idea was to remove the carbon and phosphorus from the raw material leaving a commercially pure iron, that could be forged or rolled into an endless variety of shapes. Over the years the process has been refined but the job was still a sweaty strength-sapping experience. The product of the puddling furnace was a rough ball of wrought iron weighing about 100 pounds (forty-five kilograms) which had to be power-hammered to consolidate it and expel the surplus 'slag' before it could be rolled.

Traditionally this has always been one of the most rugged jobs in the industry and the men that were employed thus were truly 'iron men'. They were hard drinking and hard working men providing a hint perhaps of the origins of the Ketley 'character' that was to develop over the next 200 years. Upon discovery of the puddlers role my great grandfather Felix Lowe, who had been a puddler all his life, immediately became the subject of great family pride and respect from a great grandson he never knew. I was also beginning to form a greater appreciation of the hardships and lifestyle of my ancestors and the part that they played in the development of the area.

REVOLUTION

Despite having been born and raised in an area that is generally regarded as the birthplace of the Industrial Revolution I confess to a lack of full appreciation of its importance, until now! Naturally we were taught our local history at Ketley school. I even recall field trips to key places in the Ironbridge Gorge but, tales of soldiers, explorers and adventurers were always more appealing than pot makers and bridge builders to young minds. Even as an adult I didn't take that much notice of my local heritage, of course I was aware of it but I guess, like everything else on the doorstep, it's just taken for granted. To most people the word 'Revolution' conjures up images of a repressed citizenry struggling for freedom in a bloody conflict and history has shown most revolutions are born out of necessity, avarice or greed which fits perfectly that image. The heaviest casualties in such conflicts usually come from within the ranks of the 'foot soldiers' and the plaudits afforded to the leaders.

To my way of thinking the Industrial Revolution of the late 18th Century was in many ways no different. My analogy is that the struggle was the race for the industrial power of steam and commerce, and the foot soldiers were the workforce, including women and children. I see the illustrious leaders as Darby, Reynolds and Goldney with the battleground as the County of Shropshire particularly at Ketley, Ironbridge and Coalbrookdale.

Ketley was plunged into this new revolution in 1757 when Thomas Goldney, Abraham Darby and Richard Reynolds decided to build an ironworks on fourteen acres of land leased from Earl Gower. The area was then known locally as the 'Allmoores' and that original Ketley furnace site is still in use today, operating as Sinclairs Ironworks. The key players in this new business were inter-related, long-time associates and predominantly of the Quaker faith.

As with all great dynasties blood and marriage bound and strengthened the 'family'. This alliance reminded me a little of the present day Mafia organisation. Thomas Goldney would be cast in the role of 'Godfather' and the others as the 'heads of the various 'families'! Make no mistake they were every bit as powerful and ruthless as the 'Mafioso'.

Goldney and, by association, the others were prominent in the infamous Bristol slave trade. The trade, which was sanctioned by the Crown was so lucrative that traders such as Goldney became instantly wealthy. Ironically the demand for ironware trade goods rapidly advanced the birth of the Industrial Revolution.

Abraham Darby the first was born on 14th April 1678, the son of a Quaker locksmith and was brought up in the West Midlands town of Dudley. Dudley was in the heart of what is referred to today as the 'Black Country' – a nickname earned through its (literally) dirty industrial background.

On completion of his apprenticeship to a Birmingham-based maker of malt mills Darby married and set up business in Bristol as a maker of malt mills in his own right. In 1702 he became a partner with other Quakers in the Bristol Brass Wire Company and began experimenting with brass pot founding. This interest in, and the demand for, iron led him eventually to Shropshire and Coalbrookdale. Ultimately, experiments and determination drew him toward the groundbreaking invention of coke smelting. Thomas Harvey, who had been a partner in the 'Bristol Brass Wire Company' married into the family to become Darby's brother-in-law. Upon the death of the first Abraham Darby in 1717 Harvey, Thomas Goldney II and Richard Ford, another son-in-law to the Darby family, ran the business until Abraham Darby II, who was only six when his father died, could take over in 1728. Continuing the family links Darby made Richard Ford II his clerk of the company. Abraham Darby II died suddenly in 1763 at the age of fifty-two and his son-in-law, Richard Reynolds took over.

Richard's sons William and Joseph eventually succeeded their father ensuring the continuance of the dynasty. Richard had made a great deal of money but was very generous and is reputed to have given away £18,000 in one year for the relief of the poor in London. He had a shrewd feel for the local Ketley community, financing a school, believed to be the first in the area.

As an incentive he offered his workers extra money if they allowed their children to attend. Richard was a sincere benefactor to the local residents. Each year he played host to the local children at his 'Bank House' home in Ketley (now part of Ketley Bank).

This special day became known as 'gooseberry day' and an early newspaper report records the occasions as 'a great frolicking time with the gathering and eating of the fruit from the Reynolds orchards was enjoyed by the little ones'. Despite their generosity, these men were as ruthless and as sharp as any modern day moguls. They began buying up farms and land in the general area to allow them to control the food chain as well as the workforce. The 'Bristol Mafia's' grip on the area tightened. Traditionally miners left the pits in the late summer months for the less dangerous and far healthier work environment of harvesting, but with the mine owners and iron masters controlling the agricultural as well as the industrial workforce, that option was denied to the working classes who were now forced to work in the pits and foundries all the year round. The bosses were also drawn into the supplying of food and shelter for their new expanding

Richard Reynolds, upon his arrival in Ketley in the 18th Century immediately recognised the value of education and religion. The devout Quaker had a school built in Coal Pit Bank, Ketley that was essentially a Sunday School.
(The Ironbridge Gorge Musem Trust)

William Reynolds was particularly gifted and was responsible for the construction of a one and a half-mile long canal between Oakengates and Ketley to carry coal and ironstone to the Ketley furnaces.
(The Ironbridge Gorge Musem Trust)

work force. 'Barracks', (a terraced row of industrial dwellings) became a familiar site in Ketley and the surrounding areas. Another spin off from the farming side was the natural production of fodder for the hundreds of horses and mules used in the mines and canal waterways. The whole system completed a perfect circle of power.

William Reynolds, who lived in the 16th Century Ketley Hall, was particularly gifted and was responsible for the construction of a one and a half-mile long canal between Oakengates and Ketley to carry coal and ironstone to the Ketley furnaces. The poorly maintained road service between Oakengates and Ketley, which was constantly being churned up by the heavy coal carts that used it daily, had prompted the canal project. A letter from Reynolds to his brother-in-law William Rathbone , dated 16th January 1788, provides a rare insight into the construction. William talks of 'having my hands full with the terrain and management of the 200 to 300 men working on the canal project'!

The waterway began near what is today the Greyhound roundabout on the outskirts of Oakengates and flowed east in the general direction of Wellington. It passed under a bridge near Hartshill where the present day

The famous Ketley canal and Inclined Plane have long since gone and you will have to search diligently to discover the few frail fragments of the canals existence that remain as a reminder of revolutionary days. Here is the site in Ketley of the incline plane as seen around 1970. *(The Ironbridge Gorge Musem Trust)*

pub, the 'Pear Tree Bridge' is sited, thus perpetuating the memory of the great waterway.

The canal then ran parallel to the old Watling Street road and through a tunnel located at the Potters Bank, snaking off to the left and on to the Red Lees, finally ending at Ketley Hall. This is where the major snag for the new Ketley Canal presented itself. There was a drop of seventy-three feet at the canal's head sited at Ketley Hill, adjacent to Ketley Hall. Refusing to concede William took what would today be the obvious step.

He 'went to press' and announced a competition for 'suitably qualified men to devise a system for negotiating the drop successfully'. A pair of particularly bright civil engineers who were employed by the Coalbrookdale Company in Ironbridge won it. The extremely talented Henry Williams was a young man with a wealth of experience of erecting Boulton and Watt engines. He had worked on the furnaces at both Coalbrookdale and Ketley around 1779 with his friend and contemporary, John Lowden. The close friends devised a method of raising and lowering heavy weights from one navigation to another. Henry's design for an 'Inclined Plane' was a modification of a similar device already built at Ketley, but the winning effort proved to be a superior and much more practical design.

A Ketley Mon

With his reputation greatly enhanced Williams swiftly graduated to the post of Superintendent Surveyor of the Shropshire Canal Company where he was later to be credited with being responsible for building and improving part of the Holyhead road which ran through the coalfields of Ketley. As co-designer he was also chosen to oversee the building of the first Inclined Plane on any British canal. The site of the Plane was in doubt for many years but it has now been established that it was on the south side of Ketley Hall on Ketley Hill falling westwards towards the Ketley works. This waterway became one of the engineering wonders of the time and people came from far and wide to view the twin marvels of Ironbridge and The Ketley Canal.

The Inclined Plane had, briefly, made the township of Ketley famous. A token issued by the Coalbrookdale Company in 1792 had images of the canal on one side and the bridge on the other. Crowds of curious onlookers day-tripped to Ketley Hill to marvel at the ingenious Plane and the tokens were sold as souvenirs of the occasion. William Reynolds has been erroneously credited with the invention of the Inclined Plane, but there is evidence of a similar device being explored on the continent and the Tyrone Navigation in Ireland. The one fact that is not in dispute is that the FIRST Inclined Plane was designed and built in Ketley.

Under the leadership of the Reynolds brothers Ketley became the 5th largest ironworks in Britain. For sixteen years after the death of William in 1800 his brother Joseph maintained the prosperous state of the three furnaces owned by the family until 1816 when the company fell victim to a falling demand.

In July of 1817 a Company of ironmasters led by banker and glass maker Richard Mountford of nearby Donnington Wood, together with Henry Williams of Inclined Plane fame, joined William Shakeshaft and William Hombersly to resurrect the furnaces under the banner of 'The Ketley Company'. The shares were priced at £20 and the venture proved to be extremely successful for the next sixty years.

Upon its collapse the plant was sold to Nettlefolds Limited who effectively did nothing until 1903 when the main furnace was sold on to Duncan Sinclair.

Sinclair was a man of great experience, vision and credibility with the status of former manager of the Coalbrookdale Company among his credits. He took over the defunct furnace and turned it around. Sinclair, a canny Scot, formed the Sinclair Company with a handful of staff. The original sixty employees grew to over 200 by 1912, and the forthcoming war ensured an immediate long-term future for the factory. The historic furnace thrived and survived and, as The Allied Ironfounders, it reached its zenith in 1964 when 2,212 souls were listed on the pay roll. It's sister factory of Glynwed-Aga became famous for its production of the Aga Range cooker, renowned world-wide with a 'who's who' of clients.

The Glynwed Foundries, as it became in later years, produced the less glamorous but equally important cast-iron guttering, soil and drainpipes. Over 200 years later the foundry is still functional, rejoicing once again under the name of Sinclair. Although the workforce is down to less than 600 it is one of the few tangible links to the industrial past that remains in present day Ketley.

Fortunately for those who will follow us, reminders of this golden age live on in the Ketley place names: Reynolds House flats, Incline Plane, Quarry Lane and Sinclair Gardens. Also one of the original three man-made pools that served the Ketley furnace remains. 'Parkers Pool', named after a former resident of the area is a popular well-stocked fishing spot and a haven for endangered water fowl such as coot and heron.

The famous Ketley canal and Inclined Plane have long since gone; you have to search diligently to discover the few frail fragments of the canals existence that remain as a reminder of revolutionary days. Part of the bridge that carried the canal over Red Lees and on to the Inclined Plane still bear silent witness to the past in the few fragments of brickwork that remain.

Local folklore adds to the history of the area with tales of residents skating on a section just before Potters Bank. Domestic water supplies were still being drawn from the same location in the late 19th Century. Another snippet of local folklore relates the tale of a disastrous collapse in the tunnel at Potters Bank in 1897 when a horse was supposedly crushed and killed and the ostler badly injured.

A Ketley Incline Plane token from 1798 illustrates the head of the plane and provides some reference to the mechanism used.
(The Ironbridge Gorge Musem Trust)

THE LOWE FAMILY TREE

The impact of the Industrial Revolution was global and the hitherto little hamlet of Ketley, barely two square miles in size was at the core of the struggle.

Another little known fact taken from census records of the time, is that between the years 1780 and 1910 Ketley, which in those days included Coal Pit Bank and parts of Wombridge, was the most densley populated area in the entire county of Shropshire! I imagine that word of mouth and early newspaper reports would have alerted people of the county to the fact that men were wanted for work in the area. Miners and ironworkers were needed for the Ketley furnace and the pits that were beginning to dominate the landscape. Navigators for the proposed canal systems in the general area attracted dozens of workers including a large contingent of Irish navvies. The result of this influx was that Ketley became a bustling boomtown almost overnight.

Miners, boatmen, navvies, iron men, and ancillary workers such as smiths, ostlers and merchants bolstered the local population, making it something akin to the futuristic Klondike and California gold fields. Among the early imports came my ancestor James Lowe with his new wife Eleanor, arriving in Ketley from Wrockwardine near Wellington in 1784. They settled in Wombridge Parish at a place called Staneford, which later became known as Beveley Brook, and eventually the Beveley of today. Their first born, a son was baptised as James Lowe in Wombridge Parish Church on 2nd September 1792.

This was the beginning of the Lowe-Ketley connection with baby James being the first in a direct line of eight male Lowes born in the Ketley area. Our family tree can be traced back to the village of Highly in Shropshire. On 4th July 1694 a Thomas and Jane Lowe christened their newborn son Thomas Lowe at the local church. The first four males in our family tree were all called Thomas which is not an unusual fact on it's own, but the curious coincidence is that my grandson, who had been born in 1996, five months before my research into the family tree had begun, was also named Thomas! The name had been selected by his parents on a purely personal choice and clearly without the knowledge of our early lineage!

The James Lowe born in Beveley in 1792 married a Susannah Peplow from Wellington on Christmas Day in 1814, and in their fifty-seven years together they had at least nine children, the eldest being Joseph Lowe, my great great grandfather. James and Joseph, were coal miners all their lives, drifting between the numerous pits in the Red Lake and Beveley coalfields. Joseph married Martha Johnson who also originated from Wellington in 1836 and their eighth child, Felix was born in Beveley on

Saturday 21st January 1854. Felix broke the family coal miner mould by taking up the trade of a puddler. I was aware through my research that many marriages, christenings and burials took place on non working days such as Sunday or saints days, so I was slightly bemused upon discovering that my great grandfather Felix Lowe's birth was registered on the day of his birth, a Saturday. I can only guess that the child was perhaps not expected to survive. The copy of his birth certificate records mother Martha as registering the birth. Joseph would have been at work on a Saturday and in common with many working families of the time Joseph would not risk losing his job to personally record the birth of his son.

When I first read the details on my great grandfather's birth certificate I tried to imagine the trauma and pain of a woman who had just given birth and then making the two mile journey on a cold January day. Martha would have made the journey by the transport of the day. This was pre-railway service in Ketley, so travelling was restricted to the primitive. To travel by horse and cart on what would have been a rutted and rough road by a woman in her condition is hard to imagine and is a good example of the hardships facing the working classes of that time. Felix married Elizabeth Richards from Shifnal in 1881 and fathered six children, the third – Hubert Lowe – who was born in Beveley, Ketley in 1887 was to become my paternal grandfather. In 1918, Hubert, or Bert as he was popularly known, married his old school friend widow Emma Barnett, nee Jones, who had also been born locally in the nearby coal mining area at New Dale, Ketley. She was the daughter of a miner and her five brothers were also local coal miners.

As children, Emma and her two sisters gathered ironstone and clinker remains in and around the New Dale in the early nineteen hundreds. The sight of little children of both sexes scavenging on the pit mounds was common at the time. Bert and Emma were married at Wellington Registry Office in 1918, six weeks after their first child Dorothy Lucy Lowe was born.

The story handed down though my family is that my grandmother Emma widowed with two young boys was forced to find work at a local brick-making factory. Her job entailed wheeling a heavy barrow loaded with bricks from one part of the factory to the other, and that my grandfather who was delivering brick-making material to the factory, became re-aquainted with his old neighbour, and set out to woo the attractive young woman. He vowed that she would never push another wheelbarrow if she married him. What woman could resist that 'romantic' promise?

Bert had sworn not to follow his father Felix into the hell of the puddling sheds, opting instead for the outdoor life with a local farmer called Jones. My father Leonard Herbert Lowe was born at Ketley Offices in October 1919 and I was born at 5 Victoria Avenue, Ketley – my grandparents house – on 21st March 1943. My firstborn, son Russell, was born in 1964 whilst we were living in Broadway, Ketley and his son Thomas arrived in 1996 when his parents lived at The Rock, Ketley.

It's obvious that I am proud of my heritage and especially my family links with my place of birth. I have developed a new-found respect for the people, including my ancestors who experienced one of the most dramatic periods in this country's history. I find it remarkable (and encouraging) that most of my family members lived to a great age. James was eighty when he died, Joseph, seventy-three, Felix, seventy-nine and Bert, eighty. My dad died in 1996 aged seventy-seven.

I discovered no outstanding achievements or successes within my family research, just honest, hardworking souls which formed the backbone of the workforce during the industrial struggle of the 19th and 20th centuries.

A view of Ketley in October 1964 with development taking place both sides if the A5. Still in evidence are the pit mounds. *(Shropshire Star)*

RED LAKE MURDER of 1812

Ballad writing was a popular and conventional method of story telling in the nineteenth century, and a quietly but well-spoken bachelor named Samuel Morgan was Ketley's favorite. The poet-painter lived his latter days in Ketley Brook during the early part of the 20th Century. The son of ballad writer Jerimiah Morgan, he was a familiar figure about the area of Ketley. Most Sundays would find him wearing his trademark bowler hat as he hawked newspapers around the parish on an old homemade wooden trolley. As a sideline he would sell you a 'penny sheet' of one of his many poem-stories or his latest watercolour of the Wrekin. His work was often humorous with strong social comment woven into the storyline. Samuel re-hashed a version of one of his dad's efforts entitled 'The Red Lake Murder of 1815' which had been published in a Dawley newspaper around 1903.

Like his father before him, Sammy gathered most of his source material from pubs and ale houses so there was probably a great deal of embellishment and exaggeration to contend with. The origin of these 'poems' has its roots in the early part of the 19th Century when the workers would retire to the alehouses after a hard day's work. They would sing or recite their tales over a glass or two. I had seen a copy of the epic nineteen verses Red Lake Murder poem and believed it to be a mythical tale, but a trawl through the papers of the early 1800s revealed the story to be true.

There was a murder in Red Lake, not in 1815 but in 1812. The Salopian Journal of 25th March 1812 carried the trial transcript. It is a classic tale.

At about 7 o'clock on the cold, damp and misty morning of Saturday 1st February that year a small boy on an errand for his mother made a gruesome discovery while walking near the Red Lake Quarry.

A chance look into the pit caused the boy to flee to the nearest house as fast as his legs would carry him. The bloody body of an elderly man lay at the bottom of the deep quarry pit. When the boy returned to the scene with two local women it was quickly established that the old man was dead.

His badly fractured head was resting on his right arm. Seeing blood on the chest of the dead man, one of the women slipped his shirt down and made the gruesome discovery that the dead mans throat had been cut.

Within a very short time a ghoulish crowd had gathered at the pits side, all craning to see the 'body' and it wasn't long before it was recognised. The dead man was sixty-four year-old local man William Bailey. As was the custom of that time the dead mans closest relative was sent for. John Bailey, who also lived in Red Lake, arrived at about 9.00a.m. and identified the body of his elder brother William. Searching the clothing of his brother, John found three keys in his pockets and ordering one of the onlookers to watch over the corpse, he went to William's nearby home to discover that it had been ransacked. Money and items of clothing were missing and John Griffiths, Williams's intimate friend and new confidant was sent for to see if he could shed any light on the dead mans demise. When told of his friend's death the twenty-four year old Griffiths refused to go to the scene to view the body, claiming he had a fear of 'seeing the dead'. Griffiths became an immediate suspect due to his refusal to visit the scene and his nervous behaviour. Later one of the women in the crowd recalled seeing Griffiths in deep conversation with Bailey the previous evening outside Griffith's home.

John Bailey having had his brother's body removed to his home, went to the High Constable, a local man named Shepherd, to obtain a warrant to search Griffiths's two houses. Griffiths had recently acquired a new house which he was fixing up for his wife and family who still lived in another home a short distance away.

On the stairs of the new house they discovered a bloodied coopers adze, and a cellar drenched in blood. There was also evidence of 'something having been dragged' from the house and onto the earthen road. Eyewitnesses were pretty thick on the ground too, one person had seen Griffiths dragging a bundle along in the dark in the general area where the body was found, and another had seen him carrying hands full of sand into his home, making several trips to the nearby sand pit.

The final piece in the rapidly growing case against him was when Griffiths, who was a cooper by trade, failed to turn in for work. He had made a run for it. The fugitive was dramatically arrested as he waited at the Rose and Crown pub in nearby Oakengates, for the London-bound Flying Dutchman coach.

At 9:30am on the morning of 20th March 1812 the trial of John Griffiths commenced at Shrewsbury Assize Court. He pleaded 'not guilty' to the murder of William Bailey. There were twenty-two witnesses, including the boy who found the corpse.

The all male jury were sworn in and the first witness was called; The small boy nervously told the court of his grisly find and of the immediate reporting of the discovery to the two women. John Bailey gave uncontested evidence of identification and a string of locals told of the recent friendship of the older man by the younger, including sightings on the night of the murder of the two men walking to Griffiths new house which was as yet unoccupied.

A significant piece of evidence came from the leader of the local chapel when she attested that Bailey and Griffiths, normally regular Friday night Bible class attendees, failed to attend on that last fateful evening. Another witness told of seeing Griffiths dragging something wrapped in a sack or piece of cloth. Illuminated by the blazing light from the nearby

Botfields furnace the woman witness was able to positively identify John Griffiths. Surgeon Evans who had carried out a post mortem examination on the dead mans body gave the most damning evidence. The list of wounds included several over the left eye and the crown of the head caused by what the Surgeon described as 'a heavy instrument'. However, the most dramatic and gruesome evidence was the production of the dead man's skull and the alleged killer's coopers adze. The court was held spellbound when Evans slowly and deliberately demonstrated the exactness of the fit of the adze head and the wounds in the skull. This theatrical performance proved to be the most conclusive evidence in the case.

During the day the prisoner had remained calm and insensible to the inevitable fate that awaited him, and his feeble attempt at defence quickly evaporated with his appearance in the dock and the flimsiest of stories. Griffiths claimed that his friend had stumbled into the quarry pit as they walked in the dark, thus causing the injuries sustained.

This evidence was easily rebutted by the previous evidence of the light from Botfield's furnace, which lit up the area for miles, including the area where the evil deed took place.

The defendant's statements that the blood in his cellar was the result of him cutting up horsemeat for his two dogs, and the possession of a shirt, money and watches belonging to the dead man which, he claimed were gifts, also were easily discredited.

The Judge summed up, drawing the jury's attention to the precise marks on the skull and the various sightings of the former friends on the fateful night.

The jury didn't even leave the court; they huddled together for a few moments and then the foreman rose to solemnly return a verdict of "Guilty".

Black-capped, the Judge gave the customary address and passed down the dreaded sentence of death. Finally, the realisation of his awful fate hit Griffiths at last and he was taken, shaking and distraught, to the cells below the court. The time was 5.30pm. Exactly eight hours after the trial had begun!

In the dank cold dungeon Griffiths sobbed and asked to see the Chaplain. He showed penitence and confessed to having perpetrated the horrid crime.

When the news of the verdict reached the Ketley area, especially Red Lake, hasty arrangements were made to travel the thirteen miles to Shrewsbury on the following Monday to see justice done at the public execution. The local paper reported that hundreds of spectators had arrived for the mid-day execution, many from Ketley where the crime was committed.

Special dispensation had been granted by the chartermasters for time off work in the Ketley coalfields and furnaces.

A Ketley Mon

This view from Red Lees looks towards Red Lake, the scene of the 1812 murder. The picture was taken in 1906, though little had changed in between. *(Alan Harper collection)*

After receiving the Sacrament Griffiths took his last few steps as he ascended the gibbet at twelve noon precisely. He sang the popular hymn, 'O For A Thousand Tongues to sing My Great Redeemer's Praise' and then made his final address to the crowd. He began by warning the good citizens of 'falling into sin' as he had done, and then was suddenly launched mid-sentence into eternity.

Following what was described by the paper as, 'the usual time for public display' the body of Griffiths was cut down and taken away for dissection. Exactly fifty-one days after killing his 'friend' Griffths was (literally) no more.

This case gives a unique insight into the discovery, investigation and final despatch of a major crime in the years before the formation of the first organised police force in this country, which was over twenty years away.

The enforcement of the law was mostly under the Common Law system putting the onus on the community to assist the locally appointed constable, beadle or magistrate in the gathering of evidence and apprehension of offenders.

As a former police officer I am convinced that Chief Constables of today would be more than envious of the communities deep involvement solving the Red Lake Murder. No modern-day neighbourhood watch could have done more.

Morgan's epic poem is reproduced here in the language and spelling of the day.

THE RED LAKE MURDER OF 1812

By Samuel T. Morgan.

To all that take an interest in native tale or lore
This narrative I here relate of ninety years or more.
From out of grey and misty past fresh interest to awake,
I rearrange this record strange, the murder at Red Lake.

Griffiths the cooper from Old Park at dusk to Red Lake wended
Purpose had he to seek a loan for scheme or need intended.
Kind Bailey listened to his case with thoughtful condescension
Not dreaming treachery was at work, and murder the intention.

A fireside chat, a glass, a pipe, then did the business follow,
And Bailey took his friend upstairs, his friend so false and hollow.
And then to lend him from his store produced his money box.
'Hark'! Says the cooper, 'it is late. Tis midnight by the clocks'.

Then pocketing the borrowed gold, he said, 'twill soon be day,
And Brother Bailey. 'ere we part, we will as usual pray',
And kneeling down as oft before, both member and class leader,
Approached the heavenly throne of grace through the great interceder.

That was the hour and power of sin, the coopers cup was filling,
And murder tipped it to the brim, for he was bent on killing.
Arose from prayers 'adown the stairs, Bailey in front descended
And not a shadow crossed his mind of the villainy intended.

The cooper's adze uplifted high, 'till now so slyly hidden,
With murderous hate on Bailey's pate with dreadful force was driven.
Then Griffis', in the silent night, the dead man's house did plunder
Of valuables and money spoils, he wished to make no blunder,

In Bailey's clothes he dressed himself, the corpse so cold and cloddy,
He tied within a ready sack, to hide from everybody.
So to the quarry's gloomy edge he stumbled with his load,
His guilty conscience urged him on, and fear supplied the goad.

He stopped to listen, gaze about, with feelings wild and dread,
Of fears within and horrors round, and this burden of the dead.
The corpse rolled down the quarry side, then all around was peace,
But the conscience of the guilty man cried blood, and would not cease.

For neighbour, brother, Christian friend, he'd found this grave of stone;
And heaven decreed the savage deed should surely dig his own.
Then Griffis' turned and stole away from the quarry at Red Lake,
But midst the villagers asleep, one woman was awake.
Ironing all night with open door, she heard and saw some form,
Slink thro' the light from her cot shown, with a burden in the dawn.

The scene is changed, 'tis early dawn and in the rugged dell,
A throng of people gathered see, and still the numbers swell.
The murders out-the dead is found, the sack has been untied.
And the hidden deed exposed to view it vainly sought to hide.

Soon neighbours ask, 'where's Griffis' now'? 'How is it he's not here'?
'He should have been among the first, to see his friend so dear'.
And someone called to tell him that his mate was murdered when,
He said in the strangest manner, 'I don't care to see dead men'.

The scene is changed 'tis sunny morn upon the Shifnal road,
And the Flying Dutchman's merry horn signals the waiting load.
Down the steep bank, near Oakengates the great coach comes in view,
With horses sprite and harness bright, coachmen and guard in blue.

Some passengers, maybe alight here near the Rose and Crown,
But one among the number there casts furtive glance around,
And eagerly steps to board the coach, but a hand falls on his shoulder,
And as he turned himself about, his hearts blood runs much colder.

'Oh no offence, no offence' the cooper turned said gaily,
'No, no offence' says the constable, 'only you have murdered Bailey'.
'You're in a noose that can't come loose, you're scheming all is undone,
You are my prisoner, come along, I've stopped your trip to London'.

The scene is changed. In Shrewsbury goal, the death bell is slowly tolled,
While the prison chaplain offers prayers for the soon departed soul.
The dread procession duly formed moves toward the fatal spot,
Where Griffis' from his final lift, will get his final drop.

A thousand faces upward turn to see the guilty man,
A sudden hush, a shudder dread, thro' that vast concourse ran.
As the condemned his crime confessed. His guilt to all proclaimed,
Acknowledged pardon found through Christ, and peace with heaven obtained.

He gave his hymn out on the drop as all the people gaze;
'Oh for a thousand tongues to sing my great redeemer's praise'.
He breaks the power of cancell'd sin, he sets the prisoner free,
His blood can make the foulest clean', then Griffis', where was he?

Stern justice drew the sudden bolt in the middle of the song;
The penalty had come at last, and the murderer was hung.
The power of gold, oh who can tell, it's range for good or evil.
For which a man will sell his soul, and barter with the devil?

How great a blessing, greater curse, as hearts of men may sway;
'Twill brighten life or hasten death, so watch as well as pray.

[Poem by Mr. S.T. Morgan of Ketley Brook in 1909]

THE CINDERLOO RIOTS

The lack of even the most elementary safety precautions at most pits, together with poor pay and conditions only served to heighten the miners militant approach evolving into a winter showdown in the early 1820s.

In 1821, on a cold wintry February morning, miners from all around the areas of Ketley, Stirchley and Dawley, many of them black-faced and wearing dirty patched and ragged clothing, made their way to the pitheads of Madeley, in what was clearly a pre-arranged tactic. As with many of these 'seemed like a good idea at the time' cases, a handful grew quickly into 100, then 500 moody, disgruntled workers. Gathering support as they marched, men left working pits and armed themselves with clubs and other makeshift weapons. At the height of the demonstrations an estimated 2,000 armed men stormed forward as an unstoppable force. Engines, pit ropes and tools were destroyed as the mob gained confidence.

Meanwhile breathless riders had galloped into the Wellington Barracks to appraise the High Constable Barber and the Commander of the Wellington Yeomanry, Colonel Cludde, of the gravest situation occurring just a few miles south of the town. At about 1.30pm. the Yeomanry Cavalry formed up in their distinctive scarlet uniforms and brass helmets at the Wellington Barracks ready to ride off to quell the riotous miners. As the opponents faced each other in the neighbouring mining town of Dawley there was a moment of silence, broken only by the snorting of horses and clanking of metal from the soldiers' sabre scabbards.

Clinker (a type of unrefined coal) was the miner's main weapon. A piecing yell from the ranks of the miners shattered the silence and all hell broke loose.

Yeomen charged and slashed at the miners, intent on capturing the ringleaders. The workers replied with a hailstorm of clinker, unseating many horsemen. Within seconds several men lay wounded, some seriously. Cludde gave the order to fire and during the next few minutes a local miner, William Bird was killed outright and Thomas Gittins, from Trench, fell mortally wounded.

Many more received serious wounds and defeat for the mob looked imminent. Yeoman David Spencer from Trench Lock was wounded when his pistol accidentally discharged in its holster, sending the ball deep into his knee.

Depressed, resentful and still angry the miners gradually drifted away, taking their wounded with them, unaware at the time that they had planted the seeds of a movement that would grow and benefit thousands of others who would follow.

Bloodstained riders made their weary way back to barracks with the realisation that they had been in a hell of a fight.

A month later, on 25th March, Thomas Palin, James Eccleshall, John Grainger, Christopher North, John Payne, Robert Wheeler and Samuel Hayward who had been captured at what had now become know as 'The Battle of Cinderloo', were tried at the Assize Court at Shrewsbury, charged with 'Felonious Riots'. The penalty if convicted could be death. Thomas Palin and Samuel Hayward were found guilty and sentenced to be hanged, and the rest received nine months hard labour. Samuel Hayward won a reprieve and was also sentenced to nine months hard labour, but Palin was executed on Saturday 7th April the same year in front of the local gaol with his body left on display for the 'usual time'.

An Inquest on the deaths of Bird and Gittins returned a verdict of 'Justifiable Homicide carried out by the State'.

In complete contrast, the Yeomanry received a letter from the Secretary of State, Lord Sidmouth commending their gallant actions. 'Cinderloo' had shown the workers the way forward. It's true to say they had lost in terms of casualties, but they had proved a new solidarity within their ranks, a step that would prevail for over 100 years. Naturally tough and resilient through their very existence local miners, together with miners from all over this country, were spearheading the new revolution. Now they were fighting for a living wage and decent working conditions.

It was inevitable that further disturbances would occur. Not many people, including my fellow Ketley-born friends will know of another great riotous disturbance in the heart of our mining town!

In the year of 1842 there was massive unemployment throughout the county. Well over a million people were in receipt of 'poor relief', a phrase despised by the passionately proud working classes.

As usual the workers bore the brunt of the problem, especially here in the Midlands. Facing wage reductions in an already poorly paid industry, a year of discontent was looming large.

By early summer that year the depression had begun to bite even harder. A lack of work forced proud people into begging for food and discontent gave birth to another clash with the authorities. Workers were driven to stealing and poaching to survive.

The 20th July 1842 was a hot day. Gangs of neighbouring Staffordshire miners marched in militant mood across the border into Shropshire, reaching the town of Wellington by mid-day. Angry, and with their ranks swelling as they marched, the inevitable happened. Rebel miners began sabotaging local pits by cutting ropes and lifting gear. They stormed through Wellington town and headed for Hadley and the mining town of Oakengates, causing further mayhem en-route. Many working miners were left trapped at the bottom of damaged mines and the local police force clearly couldn't handle the situation, so the South Shropshire Yeomanry was, once again, summoned.

The flash point came as the mob stormed through Ketley smashing equipment at the numerous pits that existed in that area.

An eyewitness at the time described the scene in the Coal Pit Bank area of Ketley as 'carnage'. As the mob swept passed 'Bank House', the former residence of Richard Hartshorne and Richard Reynolds, their ranks were estimated to be 300. The rioters were intent on stopping work at the pits between the Bank House and the schools, but were taken by surprise as police, armed with pistols and swords, rushed up the pit mounds. In a very skilful manoeuvre the police sent most of the mob helter-skeltering down and away into the darkening night. Many of the rioting miners fled to nearby Wellington to mingle with the evening market crowds, while others licked their wounds and retired to their homes. The next day the Yeomanry marched from Shrewsbury to the troubled area, forcing striking miners to return to work.

The peace was short-lived. Approximately one month later miners caused pits to be idle for two weeks and the authorities were compelled once again to employ strong-arm tactics to drive the men back to work, but at a great cost to resources and finances.

The pattern had been set and the fight went on with sometimes fatal consequences.

A young Red Lake miner called James Churm, together with other local militants, joined with brother workers at the 'Black Country' mining area of Walsall. James Churm and two men from the Walsall area drowned in a violent clash with the local police.

The whole affair was shrouded in mystery and at an Inquest held in West Bromwich the deaths were recorded as 'accidental'. There was much talk of a police cover-up at the sombre funeral of James Churm who was buried at his local Parish Church in Red Lake. The black, plumed horse-drawn hearse hauling the open coffin was followed by hundreds of mourners, predominantly fellow miners, in another massive show of solidarity. Grown men wept openly at the morbid sight of the young miner in his coffin, adding an even greater sorrowful note to the occasion.

The early days of the 19th Century highlighted the huge gulf between the workers and the so-called, ruling classes. The popular view of the rich was that miners in particular were a race apart, reckless drunkards who spent their spare time brawling, gambling and cock-fighting. They lived in squalor and wore rags.

One observer of the time said that he had watched a group of miners who had come into the city of Birmingham from the industrial coal fields of the Midlands 'shambling down the street, looking from side to side and into the shop windows like hungry animals'. A Mrs Gregg in her 'Economic

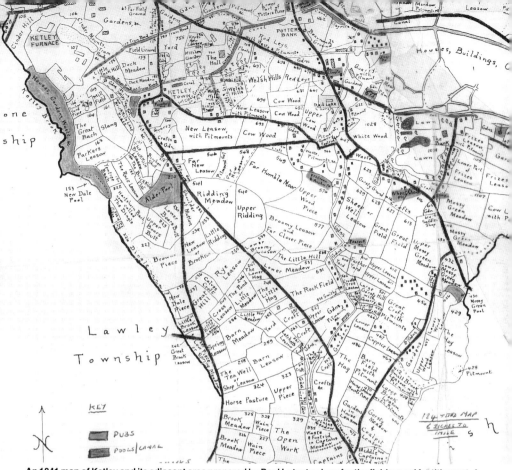

An 1841 map of Ketley and its adjacent area prepared by Paul Luter to show for the fields used for tithe rent. A tithe was a tenth part of the income, produce or profits contributed for the support of the church or clergy. A field, shown as Dock Meadow, to the north-east corner of the map is referred to in the next chapter.

History of Britain' had observed at the time, 'The miner lived less like a civilised man than a savage'.

Ignored or otherwise un-noticed by the upper classes were the daily tragedies that occurred in the pits and factories that they controlled or owned.

Hundreds of souls perished yearly through terrible accidents. Newspaper reports told of deaths from gassing, drowning, burning and pit collapses. The workers were also prone to long-term afflictions such as rheumatism, bronchitis and other muscular and respiratory diseases, which were written off as occupation hazards!

The true sadness is that the majority of casualties were children, some as young as five years old were forced to work as ironstone gatherers or surface coal pickers.

PIT DISASTERS

A prime example of the everyday dangers at the pithead exists within my very own family tree.

The Lilleshall Company employed Jabez, the youngest brother of Joseph Lowe, my great great grandfather, as a miner at one of their Ketley pits.

At twelve years of age he was considered a 'working man' but his youthful exuberance and boyish playfulness cost him his life. As the pits winding gear lowered him down the shaft young Jabez Lowe, who had the habit of swinging from the chains, was whistling happily as he descended. Suddenly the boy became entangled in the heavy chains and tragically his cry for help was not heard as he suffered terrible injuries to his lower body. He later died from his wounds.

Despite the lack of adequate safety precautions the company were blameless because this practice was strictly forbidden.

In those days hundreds of families scratched out a living by mining surface coal in and around the larger pits in the coalfields. One such family was the Frosts at New Dale, Ketley. Richard and Sophia Frost had eight children with another birth imminent. A religious and industrious family they were content with the yield of coal from their little pit. The result of their hard work enabled the large family to live a fairly comfortable existence.

At daybreak on Saturday 9th March 1839 Richard descended into his pit and sometime during the early morning he sent a workwoman to fetch gunpowder from his three-storey house which was a short distance away. Sophia, close to confinement, was ill in bed, as were two of her boys, who had been working the previous night shift. The powder was kept in the cellar of the home for safety reasons and was brought up by the workwoman to the kitchen. After filling a jar with the amount required she then left for the pit, leaving the remainder on the kitchen table, where several small children were present. The husband and his co-workers heard the explosion but thought little of it at the time. One of the pit girls drew Richard's attention to the dusty smoke cloud over his home, and the dreadful truth dawned on the poor miner.

Racing to the scene of the explosion his eyes fell upon a sight of what could only be described as 'utter carnage'. The mother and two sons asleep upstairs had been blown from their beds, but amazingly suffered no serious injuries.

Two daughters, Elizabeth aged fourteen, and Mary Ann, ten, had died instantly.

Twenty-one months old John was killed and four-year-old Richard died ten days later. The couple and their surviving children were inconsolable. The incident attracted tremendous local sympathy; the newspapers referred to the disaster as, 'a melancholy accident'. Mr Samuel Simkins of the 'Society of Friends' commenced an appeal on behalf of the family and contacted the editor with a view to financial and spiritual support for the distraught Frost family. Simkins placed the homeless remaining members of the Frost family under his roof until they could repair or replace their home. A sad epitaph carved on a tombstone in Wellington Parish Church bears witness to the fate of the unfortunate mining family, listing the names and details of the victims.

Although the Frost's tragedy was an accident, the incidents of sabotage around that time became a recognised and valid tactic in the miner's war against the chartermasters and pit owners. Crude bombs and interference with chains, ropes and pit ponies were rife. But sometimes things didn't always go to plan, as the following story illustrates.

Saturday 6th December 1851 was a bitterly cold day in the Red Lake area of Ketley. Just before 5.30am a small group of men, shoulders haunched against the cold, trudged onto the site then known as Cow Wood Pit, Red Lake. (A new housing project now occupies the site.)

A fourteen-year old pit veteran, Thomas Rigby, was already on site and waiting for the morning shift to arrive. The practice was for a boy to descend with the first shift and on that fateful day it was Rigby's turn. Although an experienced worker Thomas still only received between six pence and a shilling a week – between two and a half and five new pence – and roughly half the pay of an adult. The chartermaster (overseer) of the pit was twenty-one-year old William Vaughan who had inherited the position from his father.

The two adult miners, 59 year-old John Pritchard and 55 year-old Thomas Hayward, were standing around stamping their feet against the cold as they waited with the boy Rigby, for the horses to arrive.

Specially bred pit ponies were used to lower and raise the workers into and out of the mineshaft. It was well known that the seasoned miners resented the younger Vaughan because of his privileged position, so it was surprising that Vaughan managed to persuade the men into descending without the horses. With the manual assistance of the other workers who were now arriving, including Thomas Rigby's dad, Samuel, who was employed as an overlooker at the mine, the process of lowering the cage began. After descending about seven yards Pritchard was heard to shout, "hold it lads!"

Just prior to that call there had been a jerk on the rope and it began slipping and then suddenly broke, hurtling the occupants of the chains to the bottom of the pit.

A replacement rope was hastily arranged over the lip of the pit and two men, Joseph Dainty and James Wright clambered down to the most distressing sight of their work mates lying fatally injured at the bottom of the mine. Thomas Rigby was barely alive so they brought him up first. His father Samuel sadly witnessed the dreadful sight of his offspring being pulled from his would-be tomb.

The boy was carried to his father's house in Red Lake where he was attended by the surgeon Thomas Webb. Thomas Rigby never recovered consciousness and despite very little physical injuries he died later that evening.

It was quickly established that the ropes had been cut part of the way through with a chisel or something similar, so the police were informed and a murder enquiry began by the Wellington police. An inquest was opened at the nearby Wheatsheaf public house at Mossey Green the following day. Despite a full police investigation and the offer of a £100 reward, a veritable fortune in those days, the murder(s) remained undetected. The incident was the talk of the district and made a prominent spot in the local paper, the Eddowes and Shrewsbury Journal. Everyone had an opinion, some suspected militant local pitmen and others fancied an outside influence, but most suspected William Vaughan, the young chartermaster.

Balladeer Jeremiah Morgan no doubt picked up on the story in one of the local alehouses and penned a little poem on the subject, accompanied by the jibe; 'You can stare and you can look, I'm Jerry Morgan spreading muck'. The piece is reproduced in the language of the day.

PIT DISASTER 1851

Come all you people far and near, unto these mournful lines give ear,
Which are most shocking to relate, of three poor colliers and their fate.
They came unto their work quite soon, not knowing of their sudden doom.
As now the pit they did descend, how soon their mortal life did end.
Pritchard, and Hayward and Rigby, two of them men and one a boy,
The rope it broke and down they fell, what shrieks and crys no one can tell.
It strikes our hearts with terrors height, in the dead hour of the night.
Some evil person cut the rope, and two were killed at a stroke.
The men killed dead, the boy alive, but for twelve hours he did survive.
For death for him as we do know, has given a sure and fatal blow.
The news soon reached the widows ears and filled them with cries and tears.
Now to the widows I would say, 'cast all your mournful grief away,
And on the Lord cast all your cares, who always hears a widows prayers'.
And to the parents of the boy, (I do not wish to pass them by),
I hope you'll cast your griefs away, and to the Lord begin to pray.
You colliers lift your hearts on high, to God who rules the earth and sky.

He only can defend your head, while toiling for your daily bread.
Some early to the work do come, perhaps before night are carried home.
With broken bones or mangled flesh, but these were seized with sudden death.
To God each morning bend the knee, and ask His grace your guide to be.
He only from the danger can free from sudden death and deliver thee.
To any person that can tell, how the sad accident befell.
They may receive one hundred pound, if out the mischief can be found.
And if they don't confess it soon, they will meet at the day of doom.
And the sentence will be given; no murderer shall enter Heaven.
May all dear friends now ready stand, ready for death's cold icy hand.
That when the signal shall be given, we all may meet with them in Heaven.

[Verses written by Jeremiah Morgan of Ketley in 1851 and sold for 1d]

In a remarkable co-incidence William Vaughan was involved in another pit death nearly five years after the Cow Wood Pit murders. The scene this time was at a different Ketley pit, named 'Dock Meadow Pit'. The present day site of this pit is an area of Ketley Town directly opposite the current Wren's Nest pub where the remains of a small pit mound can be still seen. On another grim late autumn day the horses were again not available at the pithead.

The chartermaster, Vaughan, called for volunteers to descend the pit by ropes and chains. The miners called this particular job 'working in bond'.

It entailed wading through six inches of water on the pit floor for twelve hours, clearing the way for the other miners to gather the coal. Not surprisingly the men hated it. Vaughan, becoming increasingly angry, ordered several men down the pit, threatening them with the sack.

Faced with the real threat of job loss the miners reluctantly climbed into the cage and pit girl Jane Felton signalled to the engine operator to 'lower away'.

As they neared the bottom of the mine it became clear to the men that the conditions were worse then ever that Monday morning, the pit having drawn more water over the weekend than normal. Deciding to disobey the pit bosses' orders the men shouted up to Jane to signal 'return to pithead' to the engine man. William Vaughan, according to pit girl Jane Felton, 'went into a rage, ranting and raving and jumping up and down'. In a fit of pique Vaughan picked up a 'slab' (mining speak for a plank or block of wood), and with the words " I'll kill you!" he hurled the slab into the pit.

As the slab noisily bounced and banged its way down the pit shaft men scattered for safety in the murky waters of the pit. One man didn't move quickly enough.

Twenty three year old miner Samuel Rigby from Bennetts Bank, Ketley had been hit by the lump of wood and died almost instantly.

One of the men called out, "You've killed him," and again according to Felton, Vaughan was seized immediately with a paroxysm, crying out, "Oh wenches, what have I done?"

The following evening, Tuesday 16th October 1855 an Inquest was opened at the Buck's Head public house in Wellington. A verdict of 'Manslaughter' was returned.

William Vaughan stood for trial at the Shrewsbury Assize Court in the following March. He pleaded 'not guilty'. The core of the prosecution's case rested with the eyewitnesses, Jane Felton and the other pit workers present on the fatal day.

A succession of influential friends of the young chartermaster, including the clerk of the Ketley Company works, George Wilkes, and the owner of the Company, Ketley Hall resident John Williams, attested to his good character and standing in the community. The Judge summed up most favourably for the defendant.

After twenty minutes deliberation the jury returned a verdict of 'Guilty', but with a very strong recommendation for 'clemency'. To the utter disgust of the workforce Vaughan received the token sentence of one month in prison.

An amazing number of co-incidences in this case and the previous Vaughan disaster of Cow Wood gave fuel to the locals conviction that William Vaughan was a killer who had escaped justice. Most of the community still believed him responsible for the Cow Wood disaster. There were some niggling coincidences.

Both incidents happened at pits controlled by Vaughan, both occurred at the beginning of the morning shift in the dark days of winter when horses were unavailable. Two of the deceased, Thomas and Samuel Rigby were brothers and the pits were within half a mile of each other.

After serving his sentence Vaughan did not take up to his previous role but did return to his Ketley home. His previous employers took care of his welfare and he ran a number of businesses on their behalf, including a public house at Red Lake and a grocery shop in the same area. Vaughan died at Mossey Green, Ketley on 29th December 1881 at the relatively young age of fifty-two. William Vaughan died still under suspicion of the murder of the three miners at Cow Wood.

In common with most police officers and former officers I have developed a kind of sixth sense about situations and people.

In spite of the fact that I had only read press reports of the inquest of the original 'accident' at Cow Wood I never believed Vaughan was responsible for the murders. My first instinct was that a man with a wicked temper such as Vaughan's was more likely to act on impulse than premeditation, and whoever had cut the Cow Wood pit ropes had premeditated the crime. I didn't feel that Vaughan, who had no motive for the murders, was the culprit. Intrigued I decided to have another look at the original newspaper reports of the inquests into the deaths.

Drawing a blank after spending a couple of days scrutinising the pages of the old papers I gave up. I was surprised, though, at the lack of reports in the papers, on what would have had to be, by law, an open inquest.

Any detective worth their salt will tell you that an investigation into any crime is ninety-nine percent graft and one percent luck. My one per cent unexpectedly presented itself in the pages of the March 1862 Journal! Searching for information on another matter, a sub-headline on the back pages suddenly screamed out at me!

The headline read, 'CONFESSION OF A MURDERER'. Intrigued I decided to read on. I swear that before I read the first sentence I KNEW I had cracked the case.

The report is produced here verbatim:

'A man (whose name we may as well withhold) died here the other day. (Red Lake Ketley). The man, finding his end approaching confessed to a crime, which we are happy to say, is now much more rare than formally. Having spite against one of the workmen at one of the pits in Ketley, he had cut the rope partly with the intention that it should break and kill the man, and with him, others against whom he had no feelings of revenge. Unfortunately his intended victim was not one of those killed'.

All that was required was a visit to my local registrar's office and a quick search through the deaths for March 1862. Only one entry fitted the facts; 66year-old miner Richard Pritchard who died of bronchitis at his Red Lake home on 11th March that year. Richard Pritchard was the murderer and yet another coincidence was thrown up; one of his victims shared the same surname! In all probability the deceased John Pritchard was related to Richard, although I found no direct evidence to support this.

A search through the rest of the newspapers for the year of 1862 failed to reveal any further mention of Richard's 'confession' or of a re-opening of the original inquest. The inquest would have had to be closed by law, so I can only assume that the papers failed to report the fact or had been unaware that it had been re-opened. This saga reminded me of the plot of a typical Victorian melodrama. Horrible murders of innocent victims, a deathbed confession from repentant killer who had carried the double guilt of killing the 'wrong' person(s) and responsibility for the death of a possible relative and probably friends and work mates! Perhaps the dead can finally rest in peace now that the truth is out.

The killer would in all probability have read Morgan's poem about his evil deed. The line, 'No murderer shall enter heaven' must have burnt into his soul. I felt like the television detective 'Morse' who in his final case solved a murder from the dim and distant past. I have always dreamed of announcing in a grand theatrical manner; 'And the murderer is...........'. and now I can! There was one more link in this astonishing chain of death lying in wait for me a few months later whilst researching yet another part of Ketley history.

In the early part of the 20th Century history repeated itself in one of the pits still working in the Ketley region.

The circumstances were eerily similar and the location almost in the same spot as the 1851 Cow Wood Pit murders. Even the logistics were similar in so much as two men and two boys were to suffer a horrible fate owing to faulty ropes. As in the earlier incident, two men were to die instantly and a youth to lie suffering for a few days. This time there were no suspicious circumstances and a verdict of 'Accidental Deaths' was returned at the subsequent inquest.

On 19th December 1902 brothers Samuel, thirty-one, and Elias Churm, twenty-seven were ascending at the Rock Colliery pit at about 2.30pm at the end of the afternoon shift having finished their work for the day. The brothers lived at Ketley Wood with their parents and the rest of the family. In the same cage was another pair of brothers who were related to the Churms through marriage. Henry and John Attwood were both under sixteen-years of age and Henry, the younger by a year was to die of his wounds on Christmas Day of that year.

Near to the surface of the pit the rope snapped suddenly, plunging the unfortunate occupants to the bottom of the shaft, a distance of about thirty yards.

Thomas Jones, the pit owner went immediately to the pit bottom and found the four miners alive but in a poorly condition. He ordered the men be brought up and taken to their nearby homes where two hours later the Churm brothers both died within minutes of one another. They both regained consciousness briefly to utter surprisingly identical last words; "It's the rope!" An inquest was opened for identification purposes on the following Monday by the Coroner, Mr J V T Lander who insisted on a site visit together with the Mines Inspector to personally check the equipment and safety precautions.

The Christmas Day burials of Samuel and Elias at the Ketley Parish Church, Red Lake were a poignant affair for the Churm clan with two brothers and a nephew dead on this normally most joyous of days. A total of sixteen bearers wearing white gloves and black attire solemnly followed the caskets drawn by coal-black horses.

The majority of the local community attended to pay their respects to the deceased. Henry Attwood was buried at the same church and in the same fashion a week later.

He was attended by his fellow Sunday School class pupils and in his address the Reverend Underhill asked for prayers to be said for the surviving brother John who had sustained terrible crippling injuries.

This case brought about a major change in the responsibilities of Mine Inspectors. Accidental verdicts due to corrosion of the steel rope prompted the Coroner to comment on the lack or failure of regular inspections at pits of this and other essential equipment, and a new national system was introduced. Ironically, the James Churm who had died in the drowning incident at Walsall in 1842 was a direct ancestor of the two Churm brothers who had died on this occasion. The father of Samuel and Elias had himself been crippled in a pit disaster some years previous to this one and, prior to his accident, he had five sons beside himself all working full time in the industry. This tragedy once again re-enforces the price paid by the ordinary working folk in the mining towns of Ketley and surrounding area.

The Ketley Parish Church was built during the years of 1837-38 and given the name 'St Mary the Virgin'. It is seen in this copy of an early watercolour. The noted architect James Trubshaw designed the building, which has a mainly gothic look. Built of dressed sandstone the church possessed one bell in a west tower. *(The Ironbridge Gorge Musem Trust)*

THE CROSS AND THE QUILL

A connection between the tiny Ketley hamlet of Red Lake and the court of Queen Victoria seems highly unlikely, but it exists. OK I admit that it's a tenuous link but it's a genuine one and it played a big part in the development of education and religion in the Ketley area.

George Granville Leveson-Gower, the second Duke of Sutherland made it a personal goal to build a parish church in the part of his domain known as Ketley.

Red Lake had been chosen as the site of the proposed church as early as 1826 when local industrial leaders such as Joseph Reynolds, William Lawley, and John Hombersley, together with the new Ketley Company put their hands in their pockets to raise the then princely sum of £892. In 1831 Parliament passed an act to promote the building of new churches which added more weight to the Dukes resolve to build a parish church in Ketley.

George's ancestors had been Lords of the Manor of Ketley since Henry VIII's time. George's father, James Leveson a Wolverhampton wool merchant had acquired the land during Henry's reign. Hard work and endeavour ensured his success and he became one of this country's richest men and, upon his marriage to the Countess of Sutherland, owner of a very large part of Scotland, not to mention the esteemed title, Duke of Sutherland. The family formed a strong bond with their tenants, marking the local landscape with a Monument built on Lilleshall Hill, which was commissioned by the second Duke in memory of his late father.

The Ketley Parish Church was built during the years of 1837-38 and given the name 'St Mary the Virgin'. The noted architect James Trubshaw designed the building, which has a mainly gothic look. Built of dressed sandstone the new church possessed one bell, a chancel, a nave with transepts and a west tower and gallery.

The Bishop of Lichfield had the honour of preaching the first sermon in the church when he opened it officially on Sunday 18th November 1838. A consecration ceremony took place a year later. Thirty-year-old Thompson Stoneham was appointed first incumbent, remaining in situ for nearly forty years.

Mary Ann Dawes, daughter of local farmers Robert and Mary Dawes, was the first child baptised in the new church. The ceremony, conducted by Stoneham, took place on 25th November 1838, precisely one week after the church was officially opened.

The Duke, who personally appointed Stoneham, also provided him with a house. Apparently the vicar of nearby Wellington Church objected to the new competition and, by a series underhand moves, prevented the new curate from holding a licence to perform marriage ceremonies for at least a year. Even after the struggling new vicar finally got his licence the Wellington vicar, in a seemingly jealous moment, insisted that the fees should be paid directly to him.

Another piece of local folklore tells of a sneaky manoeuvre by the church's benefactor when the Duke paid an incognito visit to his new parish. Anxious to discover at first hand whether 'his church' was being made good use of, the Duke decided to pay an anonymous visit to Ketley.

One Sunday, suitably disguised, the eminent visitor slipped in unrecognised by the regular congregation and later commented to friends that the service led by the Reverend Stoneham was suitably stirring, and the singing of the hymns by the worshippers was very much to His Lordship's liking.

And the link to the throne? This existed through the personage of the Duke's wife, Harriet Howard, who was Queen Victoria's favourite Lady-in Waiting.

When the Queen's Consort, Albert died, Harriet was, for a short time, one of the few people who were allowed access to Her Majesty. In fact Harriet, Duchess of Sutherland was a constant companion to Victoria for some time and George was a familiar, and regular, visitor to the Palace.

The Vicarage, which was designed by Edward Haycock of Shrewsbury, was erected in 1880 by local contractors R and J Millington.

The 4th incumbent, the Reverend John Sainsbury Cowley, became a unique statistic when he died suddenly on 15th December 1895 after conducting a funeral at the church. The forty-two-year-old vicar had a full programme that fateful Sunday.

Cowley attended early communion followed by a Sunday school class and a Divine Service at 11o'clock. Although he had been feeling 'unwell' for a few days the devout and dedicated vicar insisted on fulfilling his duties by officiating at the funeral of a 72year-old Red Lake former miner in the afternoon. Upon returning to the adjoining vicarage at 4.20pm he suddenly collapsed and died in the dining room of the house in the presence of his wife and daughter. Reverend John Cowley's funeral a week later drew a very large and distinguished congregation.

In the early part of the 1950s the old churchyard within the grounds of the church was declared full and plans were made for a second burial ground.

On Saturday 26th April 1952 the Chairman of the Parish Council, William Upton, officially opened the Red Lees burial ground provided by the Wellington Parish Council. The fourteenth and current incumbent of the church is the Reverend Dennis Smith who was appointed the post in 1993. The avuncular vicar is responsible for several parish churches in the area and has great respect and feeling for his play hard, work hard parishioners.

Intrinsically religion and education have always run side by side in the development of the world's civilisations and Ketley of the last century was no different.

Richard Reynolds, upon his arrival in Ketley in the 18th Century immediately recognised the value of education and religion. The devout Quaker had a school built in Coal Pit Bank, Ketley that was essentially a Sunday School. Operating only on a Sunday, the traditional day of rest, it neatly combined the twin subjects of religion and education for the benefit of its pupils. It is reported to have had up to 300 eager scholars by 1786.

A Gravesend, Kent born man, who rejoiced under the wonderful name of Shadrack Robert Thomas Pocock, was a dedicated educationalist who ran the private Sunday School in Coal Pit Bank from about 1830 to his death at age 65, in 1859.

He had arrived in the Ketley area with his wife Ellen via Bristol. Pocock had strong connections with the 'Bristol Mafia'. He was recruited by them to continue the important task of educating the local worker's children, and he dedicated his life to that end.

In an advert placed in a county newspaper in October 1846 Pocock claimed that his private school was teaching 'the classics, mathematical and commercial subjects, for twenty guineas a year' (£21) which was a lot of money in those days. Pocock was clearly targeting the children of the gentry. Upon his arrival in Ketley had formed a deep friendship with Reverend Thompson Stoneham who was, of course, another leading 'instructor of young minds' in the area. The common ground of education bonded the two men. Pocock's last will and testament reflected that firm and sincere friendship. The esteemed teacher was relatively poor, leaving only £29 in his estate. With his wife already dead he left the money to his only true friend, Stoneham.

In a grand benevolent gesture Pocock requested that Stoneham sell all his furniture and other effects by public auction, with the proceeds to be distributed among his poor neighbours. He was a well-liked man and this charitable act served to endear him even more to the citizens of the area, who turned out in their hundreds for his funeral. A school building next to the Parish Church was also provided by the Duke and placed under the church's control. Stoneham and Pocock were the only source of education in the area at that time and so they pooled their resources to produce an established Ketley School. The Ketley Parochial School, as it was named had three classrooms and in 1840 records show its annual income was £80. The money came from the £20 raised in fees with the remainder donated by the Duke of Sutherland. From these humble beginnings evolved the present day school situated in Ketley. The Parochial School became government funded in the 1870s, when it changed its name to 'The State School'. When it was closed down in 1895 it paved the way to the grand Victorian buildings that still proudly stand on the old A5 road opposite the

Mr Lewis Jones was builder of the Ketley Schools and is seen here laying the foundations. The date of this view is somewhere around 1897.
(Picture loaned by Mrs D A Jones)

White Lion pub. My family's 107-year link to the Ketley schools began in 1892 when my grandparents, Herbert Lowe and Emma Jones, commenced school at the old Duke of Sutherland's church school at Red Lake. The headmaster was John Jones, with a Miss Clara Leese as mistress of the infants group.

Three years later the old school closed down owing to lack of funds to make the massive repairs needed to the fabric of the building. Most of the children's parents could not afford private tuition so they were put to service or sent out to work.

My future grandmother worked as a pit girl for a time, later meeting her future husband Bert while working at a Hadley brick making factory when he delivered materials to the works. Bert worked as a waggoner for farmer Jimmy Jones at Ketley Town. My family tree could have been very different if my grandfather had taken the offer of emigration to Canada by farmer Jones! Apparently Jimmy Jones had decided to start a new life and urged the young waggoner, Bert, and his sister, Lucy Lowe, who was a housemaid to the family, to emigrate with the Jones family.

The brother and sister turned the offer down, returning to school to finish their education. A year later the new headmaster, Frank Anthony wrote these words in the renamed Ketley National Board School's log book:

"I commenced my duties as the new headmaster on the sixteenth of March, 1896. The Church School closed in December last having been taken over by the Wellington School Board-the present building to be used temporarily, FRANK ANTHONY."

Ketley School photograph thought to date from 1899. Pictured third from the left on the back row is William (Billy) Upton. *(Picture loaned by the Upton family)*

Further notes by the new head reveal a little of the educational system of the time:

"STAFF: *Frank Anthony responsible for overall standards; Harriet Evans, third year pupils teacher; Edwin Hammond, school monitor; Florence Lane, Art; 'Under the prevailing circumstances the timetable cannot be strictly adhered to for a while; March the nineteenth; Emily Parker commenced work this morning having transferred from Lawley Bank School; March twentieth: Average attendance, 173 for the week; no sewing lessons until the appointment of a sewing mistress.*"

The present day school was already under construction by builder Lewis Jones and, on 24th June 1897, the children – including my future grandparents – officially transferred to it. The Junior school building adjacent to the new school was built and opened in 1904-05. Frank Anthony was a progressive teacher and quickly established a key position on the county Education Board. He raised the status and standards at the little school, introducing practical tuition from local artisans. He also encouraged pupils and staff to take part in school concerts. In February 1902 the Ketley National Board School held a staff and pupil concert at the school and in spite of the wintry weather a large audience crammed into the school's main hall.

A Ketley Mon

As Presenter Reverend Percy Lees Underhill, the current vicar of the Parish Church, dedicated the first item, a moving piano duet by members of staff, to previous pupils from the Churm and Attwood families who had suffered in the recent calamitous event at The Rock quarry pit.

The first class boys gave an 'amusing' rendition to a piece called 'Heads and Heels' and the infants charmed the audience with a sketch entitled 'Ten Little Mothers'. Headmaster Frank Anthony, displaying his comedic touch, had the crowd howling with laughter with a sketch bearing the intriguing title of 'Dr. Killumquick'.

One name among the chorus line list caught my eye. 'Will' Upton, destined, as William (Billy) Upton to become a local councillor and Justice of the Peace and a true champion of the people of Ketley. The Upton family tree has its roots firmly planted in the Wellington area, with branches stretching back to the 12th Century. Present day family members claim that the tiny hamlet of Waters Upton in the rural reaches of Wellington adopted the name from an Upton ancestor. The family also believes that another distant relative sought his fortune in the Capital and is responsible for the naming of the famous London football stadium of Upton Park, the home of West Ham United.

My father, his two step-brothers and his sister Florrie all attended the town's junior and senior schools during the 1930s when the austere Percy Dunkey occupied the headmaster's role.

Mr P M Keyte succeeded Percy Dunkey in 1948 and is remembered for the groundbreaking idea of adopting a ship. Through the British Ship Adoption Society 'SS Sydeus', owned by Thomas Holte of the famous Blue Funnel Line was chosen by the Ketley school children. A special 'ship's corner' was formed in the school's main hall and the kids began a course of correspondence with the ship's company. Reciprocal visits were made to ship and school with Captain Renshaw toasting the school with the traditional sailors wish of, 'A Fair wind and a flowery sea'. This association

An arial view showing Ketley Schools around 1950. The lane dividing the schools head towards Red Lees and Ketley Hill.
(Picture loaned by Mrs D A Jones)

brought a bonus to the teaching staff in the way of spin off's to other subjects and interests, such as, topics on world famous ports, stamps and flags of the world and visits to local places of historical interest.

Unlike the majority of children I enjoyed school, I remember my first day there.

I began my schooling at the Ketley Junior School in September 1948 becoming the third generation Lowe to do so. I recall Miss Evans and Miss Rainey and Miss Wase three of my teachers with great fondness. The only school report of mine that has survived was one from December 1951, when I was eight years old.

Headmistress Miss Wase described me as a 'good reader', and I received a 'good' comment for history, geography and nature. My handwriting is described as 'untidy' and finally, Terence is a 'chatterbox'. (Nothing changes!) Although I have never been good at maths I enjoyed learning to read and art. I was an avid reader with an active imagination which I believe now is the reason why I developed a strong creative side to my character. The whole process of the infant school in those days was designed to guide children towards passing what was known as the eleven plus. Success gained the Holy Grail reward of a Grammar School place, every working class parents wish for their offspring. I failed the eleven plus, which in retrospect was, I believe, due to my immaturity and the fact that the pressure to pass effected my performance. Although disappointed my parents encouraged me to study and eventually pass the thirteen plus, gaining entry to the world of the artisan at the nearby Hartshill based Walker Technical College.

I was what was referred to by my current Ketley form teacher, Linda Mary Sockett , 'a late developer'. One teacher at the Ketley Senior School inspired me more than any other. Local Dawley man Gilbert Ellis could hold a class spellbound with his oratory skills. True-life stories of Britain's heroes and heroines are still fresh in my mind today. Using language we understood and never just reading from a book, he told tales of derring-do by Nelson, Drake, Gordon of Khartoum and the great Queen Elizabeth. The strange thing is I don't recall any tales of our local heroes such as Telford, Reynolds and Darby. I'm certain Gilbert would have covered them but lets face it, bridge builders, ironworkers and potters can't compare with explorers, sailors and soldiers when you are a twelve year old!

Mr Ellis had a plimsoll, which was about a foot long and affectionately known as 'Willie'. It hung on a nail on the chalkboard as a reminder that misbehaviour brought 'Willie' the pump into contact with bottoms. It was an effective deterrent.

The honour of being the last Headmaster at the old Ketley Senior School fell to Albert Hinsley Dodd and, in 1958, when the school changed status from Senior to Junior School, it was the end of a great era for thousands of Ketley children educated there. Mr Dodd poached the brilliant Gilbert Ellis when he left to take the Headship of the Whitchurch Secondary Modern School in north Shropshire. I was saddened to hear that Gilbert Ellis a few years ago.

I have never forgotten a most unusual history lesson taught by the unorthodox Gilbert. Marching the entire class out into the front playground he told us to close our eyes. Amid sniggers and puzzled looks he began to describe the scene as an army of occupation in 43BC prepared to move. In the next few minutes a thousand ghostly Romans marched majestically down the A5 road on their way from the local Roman Station of Uxacona to Uriconium. I swear I could hear the clanking armour, snorting horses and rumbling carts slowly passing by together with the smells of food being prepared. As I write about it now I STILL hear the Romans passing by!

I'm not sure if anyone else was moved by this unique experience but my fertile imagination had been in overdrive! In what would be the greatest compliment that I could pay to my old teacher I used a similar technique twenty years later whilst instructing young police recruits at West Mercia's Droitwich Police Training School.

The emphasis was on role-playing and theatricals. The police service called them 'Practical exercises'.

In the autumn of 1958 the senior pupils from Ketley transferred to the newly built Hadley Secondary Modern School, leaving the juniors to continue their education at the old twin buildings on the A5. William Poole became the latest head in a long line of distinguished head teachers at Ketley.

Upon the development of the Ketley Town area and the new housing estate at the Wrens Nest area, Ketley Town Junior School opened in 1966 and has now become an essential cog in the education of the local children.

Happily the two old schools are still active in the education chain in Ketley today. Anna Sydenham was appointed Head Teacher in January 1998, ensuring that the high standard of education commenced by Frank Anthony is sustained.

The 1904 school is currently home to a pre-school nursery for four-year olds and five-year-old reception pupils. The original older building now provides the link between the five and seven year olds.

As a previous pupil I'm proud to say that two of my six grandchildren, Peter Overton and Rebecca Lowe, perpetuate my family's connection with Ketley School, and with the prospect of Thomas Lowe and David Overton to follow the connection rolls on. The current staff are a dedicated bunch from the head to the dinner ladies, continuing the proud tradition started all those years ago by the man with the grandiose name of Shadrack Robert Thomas Pocock.

SAMUEL PARKES CADMAN

As we know from the previous chapter early Quaker bosses were eager to promote a spiritual involvement in their workforce by setting Sunday aside as a day of rest, encouraging the miners and iron men to worship on a regular basis. Originally the workers laboured for seven days a week, but the devout leaders insisted on Sunday being designated a day of rest and worship. The majority of the working classes at that time were God fearing Christians, so it was not necessary for a force-fed religion policy. It is on record that a Wesleyan Minister was preaching at the Rock Chapel in Ketley from as early as 1813 and soon other chapels began springing up all over the area. At this time Methodists, mainly the primitive Methodists, were the only Non-conformists to be successful in the Ketley area and their growth was prolific. Other religions existed including, not surprisingly, a small band of Quakers at a meetinghouse in Coal Pit Bank, near the home of Quaker boss Richard Reynolds. Welsh Baptists gathered at Mossey Green but, for some reason, it was the Weslyans that made the biggest impact.

From within the coalfields of Ketley emerged a man destined to become perhaps its most famous son of the last century, and probably of all time!

There is an entry in the United States of America dictionary of Who's Who that reads as follows; *'Cadman, Samuel Parkes, clergyman. Born December 18th 1864 in Shropshire'.* An impressive string of American College appointments includes the prestigious University of Yale, with Syracuse and Bloomington also listed, along with the titles of Pastor of the Metropolitan Temple New York, and Gold Medallist of the National Institute of Social Sciences'. He also had the coveted distinction of having had conferred on him by the King of Sweden the 'Commander of the Royal Order of the Vasa'. (Sweden 1932).

Born, as his father before him, in Mossey Green, Ketley, he was Christened Samuel Parkes Cadman at Wellington Parish Church on the day that he was born. The name Parkes was taken from his mother's maiden name. She had married Samuel senior following the early death of his first wife and the family lived in the close community of the tiny hamlet of Ketley known as Mossey Green.

The Cadman clan was a large one and, for some obscure reason, his father's sister Emma Cadman – who had recently married local man Noah Blakemore – raised the young Samuel. Although of rough mining stock there was no poverty-ridden existence for SP, as he was known by the family. They owned at least one small coal mine and a local shop but SP was brought up in a world where he had to pull his weight. His surrogate parents lived in the relative comfort of a large manor house called 'Provident House', which was situated in Ketley Bank. Following his father and his grandfather whose reputations as 'hellfire Methodist preachers' were renowned, the young Samuel entered the miner's world at twelve years of age. It was evident from the beginning that the boy would not be just another grubby miner.

As an avid reader the youngster would take his Bible to work with him and on one occasion he remarked to a fellow worker, "I'd rather go to work without my food than my Bible". His favourite reading material apart from his Bible, was the classic 'A Pilgrim's Progress' and copies of printed sermons of the great Methodist ministers, including his father and grandfather. Given his family's background of Methodism it was hardly a surprise when he took more than a passing interest in the church. His father would regularly walk from his Mossey Green home to preach at Prees Heath, North Shropshire, a distance of about 25 miles each way!

Moving to Ketley Brook in the early 1880s to re-unite with his natural parents, Samuel and Betsy, the teenager commenced classes at the Wellington based Wrekin College where the founder of the college, Sir John Bailey became interested in the talented young man and decided to sponsor him. The benefit of a first class education was to be the first step in the creation of a local legend. Around this time Cadman attended an Evangelical service conducted by the Reverend JM Pascoe at the Dawley Methodist Church. Deeply effected by this experience he was determined to become a Methodist Minister. With the blessings of his parents and his sponsor he left for Richmond, Surrey to begin his training at the Wesleyan Training College. During this period of his life Samuel married Lillian Esther of Wooding, Derbyshire. She bore him three children, Frederick, Marie and Lillian.

Driven by an inner voice that he believed came through God, Cadman made arrangements to uproot his and family and travel halfway around the world to the former colonies of America. Accompanied by his younger brother and his wife and children, the recently ordained minister headed for the 'New World' of America.

Landing in New York towards the end of the 19th Century the astute Cadman immediately saw the potential for preaching the gospel according to the Methodists among the teeming millions in the Metropolis. In the city where dreams can come true Samuel Parkes Cadman of Mossey Green, Ketley realised his dream within a few months of landing at Ellis Island.

The oratory skills honed in the coalmines of home suited perfectly the cosmopolitan population of New York. In 1895 the Ketley born preacher attained the post of the Pastor of the Metropolitan Temple of New York, which he held for six years.

He then became Acting President at the Adelphi College in Brooklyn in 1911 and finally, in 1928, his big break came when he, rather astutely, recognised the potential of the relatively new media form of radio broadcasting and seized the opportunity. Hosting what is referred to today as the, 'God slot' on a local station he claimed the distinction of being the first successful radio minister in the world.

In this role he could achieve audiences beyond his wildest dreams from among the millions of culture-starved immigrants. It is claimed that at its height Cadman's 'show' had built up a following of over 30,000,000 listeners! Drawing his audience from twenty-eight denominations representing the Federal Council of America, his replies to listeners' questions were re-produced in more than 100 newspapers.

During the early 1930s he identified the menace of fascism and declared a personal war against it, in what was a remarkable perception of the global political picture at that time. From the powerfully twin platforms of the radio microphone and the pulpit Cadman took every opportunity to denounce the Fascists Party with a venom. Affluent enough to make frequent Atlantic crossings to England, Cadman always travelled with his close family and never missed visiting home.

There were dozens of relatives still living and working in the area and he made the effort to see as many as he could when he was in Shropshire.

As an internationally famous figure he was in great demand at Methodist churches not only in the local area but also nationwide. One of his last official acts in the 'old country' was to dedicate the gates of the Ketley playingfields, a cause close to the local boy's heart. Nine months later the great man would make his last crossing to his birthplace and his final resting-place at Red Lake Cemetery Ketley.

It could be said that he died in harness. Collapsing in the middle of a lecture on world peace in New York he was rushed to a nearby hospital for an emergency operation. His loving daughter Marie supplied blood for two transfusions, but the seventy-one-year old evangelist passed peacefully away on 12th July 1936. Close friends and family members agreed that his ending was probably the way he would have liked to go. Ironically the Cadman family had pre-booked a berth on the Queen Mary for another intended visit to their homeland. Sadly that journey became a funeral cortege. Cadman's final journey began in the city of New York and the thousands lining the street paying a last farewell to their pastor, and continued on to an Atlantic crossing and his final resting place at Red Lake, Ketley. The huge crowd of church and local dignitaries stood in silent homage in the little Parish Church of Ketley, among whom were miners and ironworkers, to say farewell to Ketley's famous son.

In his later years the former miner and pastor indulged in his passion for collecting rare china, valuable antiques and rare books. Among his greatest treasures was a copy of the so-called 'wicked Bible'. This was a seventeenth century Bible that had a misprint among the text. Apparently the word 'not' was omitted from the seventh commandment so that it read; 'Thou shall commit adultery'. The devout evangelist found this a source of great amusement, revealing a rare glimpse of impish humour from the normally saintly preacher. He also confessed to a passion for mystery and detective stories with Conan Doyle's classic 'Hound of the Baskervilles' his particular favourite. SP was a prolific writer and was the author of a number of religious based books, including the critically acclaimed 'Ambassadors of God', 'The Three Religious Leaders of Oxford', and a biography of First World War English poet Wilfred Owen.

Samuel Parks Cadman seen on a return visit to Ketley for the dedication of the Ketley Playing Fields gates in 1935. Born in Mossey Green, Ketley, he was Christened Samuel Parkes Cadman at Wellington Parish Church on the day that he was born. The name Parkes was taken from his mother's maiden name. She had married Samuel senior following the early death of his first wife and the family lived for a time in the close community of the tiny hamlet of Ketley known as Mossey Green, moving to Ketley Brook.
(Wellington Journal & Shrewsbury News - courtesy Shopshire Star)

THE MAKING OF A TOWN

Few people will know of the contribution that the man known as Thomas Telford made to my birthplace. Everybody will know the name because it has become synonymous with the new town of Telford, and some may even know that he was Scottish and a bridge designer and builder. But he was more than that.

When Thomas Telford was appointed Surveyor of Public Works for Shropshire in 1787 the impact on the general area and particularly the home of the Industrial Revolution was significant. The thirty-year-old Scottish born engineer was enthusiastic and efficient in his new role. His local legacy remains with three bridges over the River Severn and a significantly massive road project carried out on the great Roman road. Charged with improving the old London to Holyhead Roman road, which passed through the heart of Ketley, the Scot rose to the challenge and during a twenty-year period beginning in 1815 the portion of the route that passed through Ketley was dramatically improved. The 'old' road passed through Ketley Brook, situated in a deep hollow. Telford took the logical step of re-siting the road in its present position above the Brook.

An ingenious man, Telford utilised the mountains of waste 'slag' from the nearby cinder hill and Ketley furnace for the new road surface. This decision neatly solved the dual problems of the basic road-laying materials and reduced the severe dip in this length of the road. The 'slag-hill' that was used formed part of the famous Ketley 'Cinderhill' which became a local demographic feature that would later be the subject of an early 20th Century post card. This rare photograph, dated 1905, provides another insight into the industrial heritage of one of Shropshire's unsung areas. Lasting until well into this century thousands of Ketley children played on its steep slopes. Older Ketley residents recall the Cinderhill with affection. The most popular pastime was sliding down the slopes on pieces of cardboard or wood, bringing a cuff round the ears from parents for wearing holes in precious clothes and boots.

The jewel in Thomas Telford's public bridge-building crown was the world's first suspension bridge across the Menai Strait in North Wales, emphasising the great man's place in the history of this country.

In my opinion Ketley has suffered from the fact that the great Watling Street (A5) divides it, effectively fragmenting the area. Although it has a town that isn't! Ketley Town was a hamlet in the area that was once part of the ancient area called Ketley Wood, though very few references are found to its town status. Lack of a Town Hall and the traditional trappings of most towns, a market or fair, a village green, Mayor or centre of local government, have placed it at a disadvantage with the other local towns

Ketley Town is seen in this picture taken in 1906. The view eastwards is looking towards the ancient Ketley Wood area. *(Picture loaned by Tony Wood)*

surrounding it. For years the residents of Ketley have had the feeling that the surrounding towns of Wellington, Oakengates, Dawley and Hadley have 'looked down' on their near neighbour for it's apparent lack of town status.

Even the most cursory look at the facts proves the town's claims to be regarded as a township in its own right. At one time, during the late eighteenth and early nineteenth century, Ketley's population alone surely warranted 'Town' status, and with the vast increase in local commerce at this period I'm amazed it never achieved it! Official figures show that Ketley was the most densely populated area in Shropshire at the height of the industrial revolution.

It is difficult to accurately measure the population at the turn of the 18th Century, but in the late 1830s, over 2,000 citizens lived in the Ketley area. The record shows that at the 1881 census around 3,000 people were living in the combined Wellington and Ketley areas, with 567 houses in the Ketley area alone. In common with other mining areas Ketley had also developed its own character, dialect and culture, which had evolved from the hard working, hard drinking, God-fearing workforce now indigenous to the area. Evidence lies in the lifestyle and leisure activities of its people.

Most miners and ironworkers had a passion for breeding and keeping songbirds; usually wild birds like linnets and finches. This tradition is still upheld by a dwindling number of enthusiasts. The miner's favourite was, and still is, a crossbred curiously nicknamed a 'Mule'. This is the result of crossing a canary and a bullfinch. Canaries are domestic birds today but law still protects bullfinches as wild birds.

The practice of 'dabbing' or trapping the wild birds originally has is roots deep in the past and is still popular today. The current enthusiasts are more likely to be licenced breeders, but there are still a dwindling bunch of exponents of the art knocking about today. One of these 'old timers' explained to me how the process worked.

A home made wooden cage occupied by a canary or a 'Seveny' (seven coloured linnet) acting as 'bait' is planted in the local gorse or grasslands, which grew in abundance in areas like the Ketley Dingle, enticing the wild finches into the trap.

When the finch flew into the cage to investigate the sweet singing decoy, a string attached to the trap is yanked by the 'dabber', which in turn pulls the entry flap of the cage, shutting it fast and trapping the prey. Not only was this a means to providing pleasant music in the drab homes of the workers, it evolved into a legitimate sport and hobby which eventually spread into the international cage bird shows that remain very popular among the old miners and ironmen. A present day Ketley enthusiast, who wishes to remain anonymous told me that 'red-uns' (bullfinches) are becoming rarer because of mans destruction of the natural habitat of the birds, for housing and other developments. I was surprised to discover that a top class Mule can fetch up to £60. The best customers were the Romany gypsies that once frequented the area in their hundreds. It's said that a gypsy would pay almost any price for an authentic Mule. Mule breeders are breaching the law but they have a genuine passion and respect for the environment and ecology of the local area.

Another traditional hobby of the miner was dog breeding. Few homes were without 'man's best friend' but the workers favoured working dogs like terriers to keep down the vermin, or whippets and greyhounds for sport and poaching. Originally it was that most ferocious of beasts, the British Bulldog. Bred for bull baiting, a legitimate 'sport' in the seventeenth and eighteenth centuries it also served as an effective guard dog and companion for the workers of the day. Bull baiting was outlawed in 1835, but in a bizarre incident two years earlier the Duke of Sutherland's agents had apparently taken the law into their own hands by rounding up and destroying nearly 500 bull dogs belonging to local miners.

The relationship between the ruling and working classes was strained to say the least. The agents, mostly thugs, were employed to keep the workforce in check and they were a law unto themselves, often overstepping their mark, as illustrated by the dog-destroying incident.

Working life in those days was extremely harsh; a six-day working week with appalling pay and atrocious conditions did little to lighten life's struggle. Through the next 100 or so years the local people developed a gritty, hard working, hard drinking ethic, which is still present today.

Alcohol played an important part in the workers life, especially on a social basis. After a gruelling shift at the coalface or a sweaty session in the furnace workers would spend what little spare cash they had in the numerous alehouses, forgetting, for a brief time, the realties and horrors of life. Through the words of a character in Shakespeare's 'Macbeth' the bard had this to say on the subject of alcohol; "Drink, Sir provokes three things, a painted nose, sleep and urine", which, if you think about it that's a pretty accurate definition!

In the testing times of the 19th Century the wit and wisdom of the bard would have been wasted on workers of the Ketley area, as it probably was in Elizabethan times. Apart from the drudgery of work the worker's time was divided between his church and his alehouse. Imbibing was the main source of his entertainment.

The public house provided the fellowship of his co-workers, entertainment in the form of balladeers and poets like Jeremiah Morgan, and drink to help him to forget the perils of work and life. Inevitably wherever there was a furnace or pit there was a pub or alehouse, and there were dozens of pits and at least half a dozen furnaces. Practically all of the forty pubs and ale shops in Ketley have disappeared over the years, declining in line with the industries, though a couple have survived the cull looking more or less as they did in their heydays. The great Watling Street was rich with coaching houses but the pride of place went to a Ketley pub. The Seven Stars was built during the reign of Queen Elizabeth (1579) as a tavern and posting station and it was later to be listed as the oldest coaching inn on the London road.

Tales of 'Dick Turpin' the famous highwayman, having slept overnight at the Stars may or may not be true – a slick piece of 16th Century public relations if you ask me!

Legend has it that the front door of the 'Stars' was the ideal size for a necessary but gruesome task! It was, for many years used as a 'laying out of the dead' board. Apparently the normal screws on the hinges were replaced with easy to remove pins for quick access!

Many a good Ketley soul took their final journey up the old A5 on that 16th Century piece of English oak. A mid 19th Century advertisement reveals some of the character of the old pub when it was up for sale by tender complete with stables, gardens and other outbuildings, two cottages and a blacksmith's shop. Just over twenty-four acres of 'excellent arable pastureland' was also included in the deal.

The pub was under the occupation of Mr S K Rhodes and his under tenants at the time and was advertised as 'Much frequented by coach and horses and cattle dealers, unsurpassed by any on the London to Holyhead Road'.

Sited on the edge of the great road opposite the Ketley Town road the old inn, complete with its resident ghost, was criminally reduced to a pile of 16th Century rubble in December 1964. The pub boasted some original wattle and daub and was awash with character and nostalgia. Its destruction was apparently to make way for a road-straightening programme! A new pub was re-built on, more or less, the same spot. The present day pub has been modernised, extended and re-named the Elephant and Castle.

The White Lion took over the mantle of oldest inn in Ketley upon the levelling of the old Stars. It dates back to 1661 and proudly stands opposite the Ketley schools buildings in almost stately fashion and is one of the few pubs left with classic features. The Ancient Order of the Druids met every Saturday at the pub for a number of years dating back to the beginning of this Century. Mable Wright and later son Albert were probably the inns most popular and celebrated licensees of this century.

The Horseshoes, which is opposite the old Ketley furnace (now Sinclairs) and the Compasses Inn at Beveley have their roots firmly planted in the 19th Century.

The Unicorn Inn at Potters Bank, which is now called the Pudding Inn, completes the list of original Ketley pubs surviving from the boom times of the 19th Century.

A map of the time shows clearly the main public houses in Ketley at that time. The Wren's Nest situated at the first of the Ketley Town bends, is on the site of the nineteenth century Fountain pub that, in turn, was opposite the Dock Meadow Pit, the scene of Samuel Rigby's manslaughter in 1856. Other pubs of that time included a pair opposite each other at Potters Bank, The Golden Lion and The Swan.

They were close to where the Pudding Inn, formerly the very popular Unicorn Inn, stands today. The Peacock pub in Mannerly Lane has long since gone, although the name lives on through Peacock Farm, which stands near the site of the old pub. The Wheatsheaf, at Mossey Green, was run by local chartermaster Mark Tipton, and there were two pubs in the Red Lake area.

The Lion was next to the Parish Church and the Red Lion was at Red Lees near to Ketley Hall. The Castle and Falcon was opposite the present day Parkside Centre adjacent to the Ketley playing fields.

With such an abundance of drinking sources it is not surprising that drunkenness and anti-social behaviour was rife in the Ketley area at this time. One of the most colourful of the early Ketley characters was a man called 'Joe Thunder'. Joe was born Joseph Hughes, in the Beveley area of Ketley where he spent his early days.

A pit accident when a small boy left Joe a cripple. One of his legs was amputated just below the knee and, as a result, he was unable to hold down a 'regular' job. Reduced to labouring at the Ketley coal wharf a frustrated Joe became an alcoholic. He earned his nickname following a police court case in 1846.

The case arose out of an incident one Saturday when Joe was 'knocking 'em back' at Mrs Dolphin's beer shop on the outskirts of Ketley Brook. A drunken Joe was asked to leave the premises, upon which he became, in the words of the constable, 'very noisy and rude'. Unfortunately for Joe the local constable, Edward Weaver was passing the beer shop at the time of the disturbance and heard the commotion. On entering the premises Weaver ordered Hughes to be quiet and quit the premises. A sozzled Joe refused to leave so Weaver called for assistance, with the result that several colleagues arrived within minutes.

Hughes still refused to quit the bar and an almighty fight broke out, ending with Joe being taken into custody.

In the Wellington police court the next day a bruised, battered and black-eyed constable Weaver stated that Hughes had become like, 'a son of Jupiter, whipping off his wooden leg and using it as a conductor dispensed thunderbolts around the pub, flooring his colleagues as if struck by lightening'. Fined fifteen shillings (75p) or a month in jail Joe 'Thunder' predictably chose to do the time.

In mid February 1848 a 'riot' broke out at the site of the Ketley Cinderhill, which was directly opposite the Horseshoes pub. Drunken Irish navvies and local miners who were traditional rivals clashed, forcing the authorities to put the militia on standby. The local police, taxed to the limit, managed to quell the situation without the military, but not before a lot of blood was spilled and dozens of violent rioters arrested.

Naturally it wasn't all doom and gloom as the following story illustrates.

The Ketley Cinder Hill as seen on a post card sent in 1906. The card mentinons a new Saturday train service from Wellington that had just commenced. *(Alan Harper collection)*

The iron and coal bosses had developed a custom called 'Reckoning Day' which took place traditionally on the sixth of November each year. Bosses of the Ketley, Old Park and Snedshill Ironworks had chosen to make that date to fix the pay and work quotas. This 'ceremony' was usually a cause for great celebration if the prices were favourable to the workforce, and they usually were. The prices had a knock-on effect because they also reflected in the other industries of the area such as the coal pits and forging furnaces. Young people especially greeted this special day with jubilation. It was an excuse for continuing the previous nights 'Guy Fawkes' celebrations.

The bonfires lit on the local pit banks were kept alive throughout the next day and the firing of what were referred to as 'petty canons' (probably a type of firework) continued throughout the night.

A local newspaper report in the early 1800s describes the event as *'A great occasion, witnessing a terrific echoing of explosions from 6 o'clock at night up to 10 o'clock with dozens of pit bank fires warming the chill winters air'*.

In the 1860s Kelly's commercial directory actually refers to Ketley as a 'township' which includes the hamlets of Beveley, Potters Bank, Mossey Green, Red Lake, Red Lees and The Rock'. Also listed were many non-denominational chapels, a national school and a post office with a Mrs Ann Williams as the first postmistress (letters arriving at 7.00am and dispatched at 6.00pm). The Post Office being designated in 1857.

The arrival of the railway on May Day the same year seemingly clinched Ketley's unofficial 'town' status.

The influence of the Coalbrookdale Company had brought the railway to Ketley, and following the opening of the line from Wellington to Wolverhampton in 1849, the Ketley branch line was sanctioned four years later. The Wellington and Severn Junction Railway built a single-track line from the Wolverhampton spur down to Horsehay and onwards to the Coalbrookdale Company.

The latest incumbent of Ketley's grandest building, Ketley Hall, was John, son of the pioneering Henry Williams. He was a partner in the Ketley Ironworks and lived a life vastly different from that of his workers. The report of the local celebrations upon his marriage to a Miss Ball in 1858 show that he must have been a popular boss.

The bells of the Wellington Parish Church, according to the local paper, *'sent forth joyous peals throughout the day, and in the immediate vicinity of his ironworks canon were set and fired at intervals'*. The corner of the Buck's Head pub on Watling Street, Wellington, had a banner bearing the words, *"Long life and prosperity to Williams and his bride."*

His company's crest and motto were displayed over the pub's doorway. All the local pubs in Ketley displayed flags and decorations as well as a number of banners and flags on the pit banks.

White Lion public house as seen in an early picture.
(Picture loaned by Fred Brown)

Seven Stars public house as it was in 1953.
(Picture loaned by Fred Brown)

The Unicorn Inn at Potters Bank, which is now called the Pudding Inn.
Shown here is the Unicorn Inn as it was in the early 1950s.
(Picture loaned by Trevor Williams)

The licensee of the Dun Cow pub in Wellington paraded a sheep through the town and then had it slaughtered and roasted it for his customers. John Morris, landlord of the Horseshoes, and William West at the Seven Stars treated their customers to a roast beef dinner for the occasion. In contrast the wedding party dined at the bride's Wellington home, where a seven-course feast was served.

Three days after the Tuesday wedding the celebrations continued with a Company dinner for 840 persons, where it was reported, 'good English fare of beef and ale were served'. Company men, Wilkes, Jones, Vaughan, Stanworth and Yardley had arranged the occasion, which included a procession from Leegomery to the Ketley Hill residence of the groom. The locally based Aqueduct Band had accompanied the walkers.

The bride's wedding dress was custom made and of the finest silk and lace. The six bridesmaids were similarly dressed in silk gowns and the groom was attired in the latest gentleman's fashion complete with silk top hat and fashionable waistcoat with fob. These facts highlight the gulf between the classes at that time.

The comparison is worth noting between a working class wedding and William's nuptials. The working class wedding would have to be on a none-working day, either a Sunday or a public holiday; Easter and Christmas days were favourites.

Although they might share the same church venue, a nominal peal of wedding bells would have been the order for the day rather than the extended celebrations John Williams and his bride warranted. The working class bride's trousseau would be probably home made and a posy of wild flowers would compliment her ensemble.

The groom's one and only three-piece suit would double as the one he would be buried in. The honour of bridesmaid would fall to a sister or best friend and the groom's brother or close relative was usually best man.

A wedding 'feast' of rabbits or fowl at a local alehouse or the couple's new home would complete the day. The following day – the 'honeymoon' over – a return to work for the newly wed pair would be a stark substitute for a trip abroad or a few days in Brighton, the choice of the gentry.

Ketley folk, depending in which part of the town they lived, had a choice of at least five parish churches in the 1800s. The local Parish Church at Red Lake was most popular, but residents of Beveley had a choice of Wombridge or Oakengates.

Folk from Ketley Brook preferred Christ Church or the Parish Church at Wellington. But most of the working classes opted for what became known as the new Methodists. There were at least half a dozen Methodist Chapels within the township's parish boundaries and the unorthodox hellfire approach seemed to reflect the harsh struggles of the miner and the iron man.

The citizens of Ketley, especially the workforce, must have been looking forward with great optimism to the approaching 20th Century. With a 100 years of what must have seemed like bondage to many of them now behind them, things could only get better, couldn't they?

The growth from scattered settlements around the old Roman road to the bustling iron and coal town that it was in the late nineteenth century would have given them the clout, both politically and industrially, to take on the challenges and fortunes a new century would bring. Many from within the ranks of the working classes would surely have been praying for an improvement on their, so far, miserable existence.

The Horseshoes Public House in a picture taken around 1960. The local Horseshoes pub's backfield was a perfect place for band practice and, of course, a handy place to quench their thirst when they finished.
Terry Lowe

Back in the 1930s, Albert Guy Bert Tranter, Jacker Rigby and Dicky Thompson sitting on the famous 'stone' waiting for the Horseshoes public house to open.
(Picture loaned by Mary France)

INTO THE 20th CENTURY

Queen Victoria ruled for sixty-four of the most exciting and important years in this country's history. Her reign has been referred to by historians as the 'Sixty Glorious Years' due to the accelerated progress in the fields of science and industry. During the young Queen's reign talented men and women were encouraged to express their skills for the benefit of Britain. As a result of the foresight of the Darbys, Reynolds and Williams in the late 18th and early 19th Centuries places such as Ketley became the rock, or more appropriately, the 'iron and coal', on which to build the bright new future. Albert, the Prince Consort, brought his Germanic efficiency and discipline to the table and inspired and encouraged numerous Victorian inventors, engineers and scientists to aspire to greatness. Men of the calibre of the unusually named Isambard Kingdom Brunel and George Stephenson would, I'm sure, acknowledge the pioneering work carried out by Reynolds and his associates as they embarked on their quest for the world's first steam ship and railway engine.

Although the Ketley Canal had virtually closed in 1805 due to the rapid move of transportation to a rail-based system, the coal and iron industry was stronger than ever before and places like Ketley enjoyed an industrial renaissance.

Sluggish canal barges relying on horsepower gave way eventually to the cheaper, faster and more economical steam engines of the railways and motorised transport.

Pit and ironworks bosses quickly realised that they could transport their product more efficiently and without the added cost of fodder for pit ponies or barge horses. The Crimean and Boer wars ensured that Ketley's main industries were kept busy throughout most of the much-loved Queen's reign.

The winds of change had begun to sweep through the country including the township of Ketley, in the late 1800s. One of the most significant changes came in property ownership and occupation. The Ketley landlord, His Grace the Duke of Sutherland, decided to sell off the part of his estate that included Ketley.

On Tuesday, 3rd July 1884, dozens of cottages and hundreds of acres of pasture and arable land came under the auctioneer's hammer. The most historic lots were the former residences of two of the giants of the Industrial Revolution.

'Bank House, Ketley Bank', built by Hartshorne and a former residence of Richard Reynolds, and 'Ketley Hall' the one time home to the Williams dynasty.

The catalogue details of 'Lot eight, Ketley Hall', provide another interesting insight into the lifestyles of the then current occupant, John Williams, and his ancestors who had occupied the Hall for almost one hundred years.

The general description of Ketley Hall is extensive and the official auctioneers catalogue reads as follows: *The property list contains out-offices, buildings, plantations and pleasure grounds, a kitchen garden, seven cottages with their own gardens and several pieces of arable pasture and other land, totalling just over twenty seven acres. The catalogue also gives a fine detailed description of the house itself; 'The House comprises an entrance hall, dining, drawing, and breakfast rooms. Study, laundry, storeroom, three pantries and a servants hall. Kitchen, scullery with oven and boiler. Coal shed, larder, three cellars, ten bedrooms, one pressing room and three attics. The buildings consist of a stable for three horses, harness room with loft over, stable for three horses, carriage house, warehouse with loft over. Third stable for four horses with loft over, and two piggeries, a boiling house and offices.*

The footnote on the auction sheet offers the following teasing information: *The foregoing is a very desirable lot, particularly to any one seeking a good Residence for occupation. The house is pleasantly situated on an eminence, with Pleasure Grounds, which are well-wooded, screening the house from general view, and is one and a half miles from the town of Wellington, ten minutes walk from Ketley Station, and about one and a half miles from Oaken Gates Station on the Great Western Main Line from which there are frequent trains to Wolverhampton and Birmingham; the railway journey from the former takes half an hour and the latter one hour.* The list of tenants included; John Salisbury Jones, Ann Phillips, Thomas George Phillips, Sarah Palin and John Lloyd. Interestingly 'Lot eight' was described in the auctioneer's catalogue as being in *The Township of Ketley*.

The event of selling off the lands, including the mining rights and property of most of Ketley was a prelude to the Wellington Rural District gaining political control over the area. This move provided the impetus for the local politicians who were working toward the twin goals of Township status and the building of a Town Hall. During this period the majority of the inhabitants of Ketley still drew their water from either a polluted pool in the Mossy Green area, or the locally famous 'Ketley Spout', a pure water spring located in the area known as Ketley Dingle. The spout became polluted due to misuse by the hundreds of travelling gypsy caravans that dotted the area.

In those days the Dingle was a vast rural area with a few isolated cottages within the landscape. The Dingle was a prime target for the nomadic gypsies with their colourful caravans. The travellers arrived at the spot at the same time every year and were mostly from the remote rural areas of south Shropshire, making the Ketley Dingle a half-way stop on the way to the annual Market Drayton 'Dirty Horse fair'.

Today part of the area is occupied by the Wellington Retail Park and part of the M54 motorway, with a tiny ribbon of grassland and hedgerows is all that remains of the once thriving Dingle.

In the early part of the new century the Wellington Rural Council extended the water mains scheme eastwards along Watling Street toward Beveley for the benefit of households on that route only. It wasn't until 1912 that other parts of Ketley began to receive mains water, and it was over twenty years before the completed scheme was in full operation. Sweeping in with the new century was a new era, with the British public facing the immediate prospect of two Monarchs sitting on the throne of England within the first decade? A further period of dramatic changes loomed.

The old Ketley Company works, which had been in decline since the late 1800s was, by 1903, completely closed down. Every local feared that the 18th Century furnace was finished once and for all and workers pondered on their future and the problem of feeding and clothing their families. The town had witnessed many highs and lows over the past 150 years but the largest employer had always been a reliable source of income. When the factory finally closed it's gates a great feeling of doom hung over the area. The new saviour of Ketley came in the shape of a hard working Scotsman who had been a former manager at the Coalbrookdale Company.

Not for the first time had that company played a vicarious role in Ketley's future.

Williams and Lowden's efforts, which helped produce the famous Inclined Plane, brought fame and fortune to the little town, and when Duncan Sinclair re-opened the works with only sixty workers an air of optimism returned.

The factory's main products consisted of light castings for the building trade. Slowly Sinclair built up the range of products and even found time to pioneer processes in enamelling and other related casting work. Within nine years the original workforce of sixty had grown to 200. Among the original employees was a Dawley born man called William Henry Bowen who had been headhunted by Sinclair to lead the enamelling system. Henry moved his young family, including son William Vernon, to a house in Hombersley Terrace directly opposite the Ketley school buildings. Bowen senior was employed at the new 'Sinclair works' as head of the enamelling plant and the family quickly settled in their new environment.

Born in 1899 Vernon, as he was known, became the first of many old Ketley people whose living memories helped provide a platform for the basis of this book.

As an added bonus for me, Vernon had been an intimate friend of my father and grandfather and was able to fill in many gaps in my own family's history, providing invaluable facts and detail. I envied Vernon's power of recall. I struggle sometimes to recall where the reading glasses I put down ten minutes previously are, whereas Vernon could relate facts from eighty years ago with a remarkable clarity of detail. He waxed lyrical about how he had enjoyed his schooldays at Ketley and recalled fondly Frank Anthony who was the headmaster of his school. Vernon told me about the structure of the school in the early part of the twentieth century. Apart from the headmaster there had been a staff of seven teachers, one for each of the classes within the school. Each class teacher taught the same basic lessons. Commencing his education in 1905, Vernon recalled using slates and sand trays to master the alphabet and his 'numbers'. Only when these basics had been conquered would precious pencils and quill pens become the norm for class work.

The school had an extensive library where reading a book a week was the general rule, of which the young Vernon took full advantage. His favourite books were about travel, and his boyhood dreams featured trips to exotic places and world famous landmarks.

Little did he know at that time but future events beyond his control would enable him to visit some of those dream locations! A progressive Frank Anthony brought local tradesmen such as plumbers, carpenters, cooks and nurses into the teaching process at the town's senior school. Vernon and his fellow pupils were taught to make crude window boxes for houseplants and basic bookcases. Ambitiously they pestered the 'chippy' to help them make a pram for one of the girls. All went well until the carpenter died a week before the wheels were to be made. Stumped by the problem of making the wheels the job was left unfinished.

The local children enjoyed a diet of the traditional sports of football, cricket and rounders on a coal 'slagheap' in the Red Lake area. Curiously named the 'footridge', this crude sportsfield was where many of the future citizens of Ketley learned the hard lessons of life. The weekly Saturday treat would be a trip to Mill Bank, Wellington and the picture house called The Picture Pavilion. The Pavilion opened in 1910 and quickly replaced its initial curiosity status as the main entertainment outlet for the local youths. Saturday afternoon silent adventure serials and cowboy and indian movies provided the staple diet for the army of youngsters who made the weekly journey to Mill Bank. Once, on their one and a half mile return journey up the main road, the Saturday afternoon football crowds pouring out of the Buck's Head ground would be treated to a free show.

A full re-enactment of the more exciting scenes from the films by the young cinemagoers would be presented by the boys, who would be mock fighting with imaginary swords and pistols, to the amusement of the football fans. The girls would be re-enacting the love scenes and swooning over the latest Valentino picture. Those that could afford a penny took the road transport of those early days of the century, which consisted mainly of wooden built waggonets pulled by shire horses. The old Roman road had always suffered wear from the various forms of transport that had used its ancient route, and the ironclad wheels of the heavy waggonets created great ruts and pot holes. The company that ran the transport was located on the border of Ketley at Bennetts Bank, and received daily complaints about the road surface from other road users, even though the responsibility for repairs now lay with the local council.

Passengers referred to the waggonets as 'bone-shakers'. A car dealership and garage still occupies the old waggonet's headquarters today, establishing a 100-year transport link with the area. Vernon had told me that horse-drawn traffic was a normal sight in Ketley when he was a boy. He recalled my grandfather, who worked at Jimmy Jones farm in Ketley Town at the time, as having the use of a pair of Shire horses and a large cart – a familiar sight in the Ketley area. Together with his brother Ernest, my grandfather hauled things like furniture for people who were moving house, and coal from the local coal wharf's at Ketley and Hadley.

Vernon vividly remembered the very first motor car he saw zooming up and down the roads of Ketley. It was distinctive and unforgettable to the then small boy. The bright red sports type motorcar was a familiar sight roaring up and down the main road then, Vernon even remembered the number and owner; Local Ironworks boss Duncan Sinclair turned heads when driving AW7 daily to and from his factory.

The local Member of Parliament for the Wrekin Ward Solomon Henry was instrumental in the building of a clubhouse for the Ketley area. Officially called 'The Liberal Club', for some strange reason it was known by the local youths as 'the Pelican Club!' My theory on the nickname is based on the presence of an unmistakable natural feature in the vicinity of the club. On the opposite side of the road was a huge bank of pennestone clay (brick making material) causing me to wonder whether a distortion of the word pennestone became 'Pelican?'

The Shropshire Star newspaper offices now occupies the pennestone bank area. The club was strictly for adults but the caretaker, who was known as 'old man Purcell', would allow the teenagers in on quiet days where they could play billiards.

The club boasted a fine air gun shooting gallery and even though the handling and use of firearms was encouraged generally, the Pelican Club refused access to the gallery to the younger members of the club.

In 1917 the boy who had dreamed about travelling had his wish granted, but not in the manner he had desired! Together with his movie-going pals Frank Bird, Eric Evans and George Wiresmith, Vernon joined the Kings Shropshire Light Infantry and headed for France to take part in the Great War.

No more mock fighting, this was the real thing! Luckily Vernon and his pals survived.

A Ketley Mon

At the cessation of hostilities hundreds of young soldiers were offered a gratuity and two months immediate home leave. Vernon signed up. Two months later the young soldier saw more action in the trouble spot of Aden where rival Arab factions were slogging it out alongside the enigmatic T E Lawrence. Following a dream posting to the old colonial stronghold of Bombay in India, Vernon found himself being shipped back to 'Blighty' via Northern Ireland. Landing in the midst of an Irish winter, he was relieved to receive a cushy job; he was placed in charge of the Bicycle Patrol roster.

Discharged in 1921he made the long journey back to his Ketley home by boat to Liverpool then train to Wellington and foot to Ketley. In common with many of his friends he secured work at the Sinclair factory as a moulder, working his way up to foreman. Marrying Edna Morris 10 years later Vernon and his new bride moved to the Rock area of Ketley and settled down to a life of domesticity. As a regular drinker at the Seven Stars he was cajoled into the formation of a committee for a bowls club on 'Grainger's Field' at the rear of the pub. The licensee, John Grainger, had arranged for the local Murphy's brewery to sponsor the laying of a green on the field. An apathetic group of drinkers assured that a quorum could not be formed and the newly laid green was never used.

The moment Vernon realised that old Ketley was finally gone was, he says, when he noticed, in the early 1960s, that the pennistone bank which stood 80 foot high had disappeared. The bank had been removed to make way for the Shropshire Star building and presses. Numerous old friendly and familiar buildings such as the Forge Row, Ketley Offices, together with pubs like the Seven Stars and the Queens Head, and the institution of the railway were disappearing one by one, never to be replaced.

Retiring at sixty-five from what was now known as the Allied Ironfounders factory, Vernon was able to enjoy his musical hobbies of playing the piano accordion and keyboards.

A devout Christian, he was a sidesman at nearby Priorslee Church for many years. The staff at the Donnington nursery home, Summercroft, called Vernon their 'Millennium Man' because if he had lived to see the new century dawn he would have lived in three centuries.

Sadly, William Vernon Bowen died on the 11th January 1999, eight months short of his own centenary and eleven months short of 2000.

I got to know Vernon very well during the last few years of his life. He lived at the appropriately named 'Lowe Court' directly opposite my home in Wellington, until his life's partner, Edna passed on. He was a guest of honour at the Ketley School reunion which I organised, along with fellow pupils, Maureen Price and Pat Ballard (maiden names), in 1992. He was also a guest at the school centenary evening.

A quietly spoken, gentle, gentleman, who, it seems, was respected and admired by all that knew him was, in my opinion, an example to us all.

In my final meeting with Vernon he revealed how much he missed his wife, he had a tired look about him and I think I knew then that Vernon was preparing to meet his God. Even though he was an accomplished keyboard player and came from a musical family he had told me that his one great regret was not taking his father's advice to learn to play a brass instrument. I had posed the question of how he would feel about the fact that he would have lived in three centuries upon the dawn of the new century. He had looked me in the eye and said, "I won't make it ". These were the last words that I had exchanged with Vernon, but I feel richer for having known him. A quiet manner and a powerful Christian belief gave Vernon an aura of 'inner peace' for which I envy him. I admired him for the way in which he had conducted and lived his life. Although not strictly a 'Ketley Mon', Vernon is very firmly an adopted son.

Children, with replica Ketley Playing Fields gates in 1935, the same year that the main gates were dedicted.
(Wellington Journal and Shrewsbury News - courtesy Shropshire Star)

THE PLAYING FIELDS OF KETLEY

The 1930s was the decade when the cultural and physical development of Ketley took giant strides, finally eradicating the odious nickname of, 'Darkest Ketley'.

The triple targets of slum clearance, street lighting and the acquisition of playing fields for the local children, were prime agenda items for the politicians who were charged with looking out for the town's welfare and progress.

William (Billy) Upton and James (Jimmy) Wormstone were local Ketley businessmen as well as elected local councillors. Jimmy and his family owned and ran a small sweet shop on the main road and Billy Upton had the distinction of running the first bus service in the area. Operating in the 1920s the motorised coach had an ingenious dual purpose. Essentially a large flat-bed lorry that was converted into a charabanc by lifting a shell with seats and fitting it within the lorry frame. At least six men were required to lift the frame into position, and out again, but the resourceful young Billy persevered with the venture until he had made enough money to open up a coal wharf in his native Red Lake.

Already on the first rung of the political ladder as Parish Councillors the friends, who were a dynamic team, worked tirelessly for their native hometown. They made it a personal mission to provide the children of Ketley with an area where they could play in safety, and had vowed to provide a Town Hall for the Parish. An informal meeting between these two pals and a small band of close friends, including Percy Dunkey the local schoolmaster and school governor John Salisbury Jones resurrected the idea of a playing fields movement. There had been an abortive attempt at this project in 1931 by other concerned Ketley residents, but apathy had doomed it to failure. The primary reason for the movement was to get the children away from the deadly and dangerous main road where, with the increase of motor vehicle traffic, a number of serious accidents – including the death of a small child – had occurred.

The first small public meeting was held at the Mount Zion Chapel on Potters Bank with Wormstone as Chairman and Upton as Secretary. On that April 1934 evening there was only one resolution and that was, 'to procure playing fields and a Town Hall'. The playing fields project eventually matured but Ketley never got its 'Town Hall'.

On July 9th 1957 George and James Beddow of Red Lees handed over to the trustees of the newly-formed, 'Ketley Good Companions Club', a piece of land next to the Ketley Junior School building. The benefactors even cleared and prepared the ground. Between 1957 and 1961, when it was officially opened, a substantial brick building was erected. This was the nearest Ketley got to a Town Hall.

The Ketley Good Companions Club is still in existence today. Their break with the original building came a few years ago with the advent of rising fuel costs. The thriving group now meet at the Parkside Centre at The Ketley Playing Fields each Wednesday lunchtime. Membership is by invitation only and the club is run purely for the benefit of, and for, Ketley people. The clubs roots had evolved from the post Second World War group that met weekly at Mount Zion Chapel, which had been formed as a war aid-based charity project.

The resolution that had been endorsed at the original Playing Field meeting produced a working committee, which was made up of the persons present on the night.

As early as 1931 the area selected for the playing fields had been earmarked. Sailsbury Jones, Billy Upton, Jimmy Wormestone and Percy Dunkey had already identified and inspected a six-acre site on 'Graingers field' at the rear of the Seven Stars pub. The ground, which had been named after a 19th Century landlord of the pub, was in the ideal area and of a suitable size. The cause caught the imagination of the people and donations of all sizes began filtering into the coffers. Local benefactors Mr and Mrs W D Van Homrigh pledged one hundred guineas (£105.00), Van or W D as he was sometimes known, had been a clerk at the Sinclair Iron works in Ketley and had married the widowed Mrs Duncan Sinclair. She had sold the factory and the couple retired to a philanthropic lifestyle. As a staunch supporter of Ketley, Mr Van Homrigh was elected president of the movement at the second meeting.

Other prominent Ketley citizens who joined the fight included James Clay of the Wrekin Foundry works and Clement Adey, a local farmer, who provided practical help, in addition to monetary assistance. He built and supplied the benches and stages used for public meetings and outdoor rallies.

Fundraising had commenced in earnest and the first money that was raised publicly came from a concert held in the Red Lake Institute building, where a large and enthusiastic audience enjoyed the singing and the talents of the local children. The committee managed to squeeze money out of the local council and the local and national playing fields associations, in the form of grants. Gathering momentum the committee hit on the ideal way of involving the majority of the Ketley public.

The Ketley Carnivals were born out of the quest for a playing field and they proved to be a great draw and a permanent feature in the town for the next twenty-five years.

That first Carnival and Sports Day on a sunny Saturday in July 1934 drew over eighty entrants in the grand procession, including twenty tableaux and numerous foot and bicycle displays. The Lilleshall Collieries

Band and a group of Ketley school children carrying a 'Playing Fields' banner led the merrymakers on a route from central Ketley to Oakengates, Hadley and back to Grainger's Field.

Meanwhile the Chairman of the Wellington Rural Council, Jabez Barratt, who was an undertaker from Mannerly Lane in Ketley, was fighting on the other front. From the battleground of the council chamber he launched his campaign for the twin targets of a sewerage scheme, clearance of the slums and the building of new houses and adequate street lighting for 'Darkest Ketley'. The impact was amazing!

By 1934 the first streetlights were in place and the sewage and slum clearance programme had begun. At the end of the previous century Ketley campaigners had targeted the dangerous main road for desperately needed street lighting. A scheme for voluntary contributions from the public collapsed at the imminent break out of the First World War.

In the autumn of 1934 the unenviable title of 'Darkest Ketley', which had been bestowed many years previously, disappeared overnight with the switching on of the fifty street lamps which resulted in a blaze of light on the main road through Ketley.

The new lights spread from the top of Potters Bank to the border with Wellington at Bennetts Bank. In a bizarre move, the petty minded Wellington Council blanked out the half of the last street light so it wouldn't shine on the Ketley side! Presumably because they were paying the bill!

With the land bought and paid for, a grandiose pair of gates were acquired, and the provision of swings, slides and sports ground added up to an extremely successful campaign begun by that great Ketley double act, Upton and Wormestone!

Billy Upton conjured up one more coup when, on Tuesday 10th September 1935, he produced a distant relative, Dr Samuel Parkes Cadman, as guest speaker at the event billed as 'Ketley's Red Letter Day'. The dedication of the playing fields gates by the world famous Ketley-born Cadman ensured maximum publicity.

The wooden platform provided by local farmer Clement Adey literally buckled under the weight of the 'big guns' that occupied it.

Apart from the guest of honour, representatives from the national and local playing fields movement and at least two prominent vicars, national and local educationalists and numerous politicians were present. The distinguished audience rose when the Reverend Harry Wilson, the then vicar of Ketley led them in the singing of the hymn, 'All people that on earth do dwell'. Reverend Harry Reginald Arthur Wilson, who came from Australia in 1921, paid a well-deserved tribute to Upton and Wormstone calling on the Nation to recognise their great achievement, and then it was Cadman's turn.

Ketley Carnival of 1938 included a float of 'The Seven Dwarfs'. 'Happy' (Bobby Austin) is second from the left
(Wellington Journal and Shrewsbury News - courtesy Shropshire Star)

A hush fell over the crowded field. Using to perfection his great oratory and showbiz skills he began slowly and quietly commanding attention by his very presence. Thanking the movement for honouring an old resident of the neighbourhood to dedicate their new gates he echoed the Reverend Wilson's word of praise for the playing fields movement leaders. Focusing on the children present, he addressed them directly by pointing out the importance to their young lives of the vital step that had been taken on their behalf with the provision of the new playing fields.

In jingoistic mood he told them that they were not only the future of England but they were the future of the British Empire, and that Britain was one of the best countries in the world to live in. The older people present had had their day he told them, and they had made a mess of it and he hoped that this new generation would do better. The old evangelist was back in the pulpit and pulling out all the stops.

He even had time for a joke. *"You should put the same energy into your play as into your work. I don't mean that when 30,000 souls congregate around a football field working their mouths and watching twenty-two*

Ketley carnivals had spawned and inspired at least one local Jazz Band, in the form of the 'Ketley Shamrocks'. The carnival tradition guaranteed one day of fame each year to a local girl who bore the by now traditional red carnival cape and the title, 'Ketley Carnival Queen'. In this 1943 picture, members of the Shamrocks Jazz Band, who were mainly Avenue residents, are seen. The drummer boys in front are Billy Hall, Graham Corbett and Lenny Corbett. *(Picture loaned by Tom Chappel)*

others, that you are getting full physical development!" There were spontaneous roars of laughter at this. Moving in for the kill, he invited all the children present to raise their right hands. A forest of tiny hands shot into the air. He then coaxed the children into repeating *" I promise to always 'play the game'."* Dr Cadman returned to his seat to thunderous applause.

Reverend Harry Wilson was clearly moved, telling the gathering that he was, 'proud to be in the same neighbourhood that the good Doctor had come from' and that he 'felt privileged to be present at such a stirring speech'.

Mr J T Kearton, who was guest councillor from the neighbouring parish of Hadley, echoed Wilson's words, declaring himself to be 'an old Ketley lad' who would still do anything he could for his birthplace, and then as if remembering who he represented, gave an official congratulation from his parish.

A unique feature of the proceedings was the erection of a model of the gates, made by the children from Ketley School under the supervision of Mrs Upton and a teacher called Mrs Richards. The model was erected to the singing by the children of 'Builders of the new city' Each of the six sections of the model contained a one word message, which was as follows;

FREEDOM. HOPE. DUTY. LIFE. HEALTH. SAFETY.

The final cost of the newly acquired playing fields came to the then princely sum of £420.00. The movement, combined with the forthcoming war, created an unbreakable bond in the spirit of the Ketley residents. The Playing Fields Movement and annual carnivals continued after the Second World War.

By the end of the nineteen-thirties slum clearance was well underway, with new housing at Broadway, (this site abuts the playing fields and the private builders had posed a brief competitive threat to Upton and company during their push for the playing fields). The Victoria Avenue, Sinclair Gardens, and Castle View, Red Lake projects were either completed or being built.

The carnivals had spawned and inspired at least one local Jazz Band, in the form of the 'Ketley Shamrocks. The carnival tradition guaranteed one day of fame each year to a local girl, who bore the by now traditional red carnival cape and the title, 'Ketley Carnival Queen'.

On most occasions the old tradition of 'May Rose Queen' was combined with the carnival Queen celebrations. A glance through the names of the early Queens reads like a list of Ketley's very own 'who's who' in the beauty stakes; Josephine Harper, Gwen Hammond, Norah Parton, Hazel Woollam, Betty Lloyd, Kitty Lane, Janet Davies, and Pamela Barber.

The playing fields officially closed its newly-acquired gates during the period of the Second World War, in line with most other towns and villages throughout Britain. Every spare piece of land had to be used for vital crop growing. The happy sounds of children at play were suddenly replaced by dozens of spade and fork wielding locals 'Digging for Victory'.

The gates were officially re-opened for a demobilisation carnival in 1946, when fourteen-year-old Beryl Mitton was crowned as Victory Queen and Gloria Parton as Carnival Queen.

KETLEY AT WAR

The First World War was a non-conscript war where the government relied upon the patriotism of its citizens to volunteer their services. Consequently the authorities engineered a massive propaganda campaign to raise the level of patriotism.

It was common for whole streets, villages or communities to 'take the King's shilling' or 'join the colours' and Ketley was no different.

Among the first to volunteer in 1914 were William (Bill) Foulkes and his cousin from the Ketley Brook area of Ketley. Resplendent in their Royal Horse Artillery uniforms, they drew gasps of admiration from residents as they rode through the Brook in a great romantic gesture of saying 'goodbye' to their respective mothers. They then headed up out of the Brook to the cheers of the villagers and the sound of clanking brass and snorting of steeds.

They must have made a magnificent sight as they rode off onto the old Roman road to make the ten-mile trip to the Cannock Barracks in Staffordshire. Bill's brothers, Albert and George, followed the pair later that year when they joined the Kings Shropshire Light Infantry.

National fervour drove many to arms over the next four years, including a local lad who became a member of the newly formed Royal Flying Corps. Red Lake resident William Henry Lane served with distinction and survived the horrific conflict, as did the Foulkes men.

The local Role of Honour lists forty-one Ketley men who paid the ultimate price for world peace in what were the slaughterhouses of Ypres, Somme and Verdun, among them my namesake. Leonard Jones was the youngest of eight children born to Samuel and Mary Jones of Beveley. As the baby of the family his three sisters doted on him, especially Emma, my future grandmother. Quiet and sensitive, he attended Ketley school and was a regular at the Central Chapel a quarter of a mile east of the Sinclair's factory where he had commenced work as a foundry man in 1912.

In 1915 he joined the fourth battalion of the Kings Shropshire Light Infantry and after basic training boarded a ship for France.

A picture taken just prior to departure shows the callow youth in an ill-fitting uniform. The haunting look in his eyes reveals the fear in his heart, or perhaps he had a premonition of impending doom?

On Monday 9th August 1915 Leonard arrived at the front and entered the third battle of Ypres. Family history tells how the sad looking boy died without firing a shot, his head blown off by a direct hit from an enemy shell. A memorial service was carried out at the Ketley Parish Church later that September which was attended by his parents, brothers and

Private Leonard Jones KSLI, 1917.
(Terry Lowe)

Archie Green and boy assistant outside his shop around 1930. *(Upton family collection)*

sisters and friends from his Sunday School group. Leonard remains with the honoured dead in a field in Belgium.

Two other Ketley men who had been school pals joined the same regiment as Leonard Jones and found themselves sharing a billet in basic training before leaving for France with the British Expeditionary Force. John (Jacker) Rigby was what is referred to today as a, 'colourful character'. Jacker hailed from Red Lake and Samuel (Sammy) Corbett, came from central Ketley. The pair had no way of knowing that within three years one of them would be dead and the other would marry his widow and care for his children and have seven offspring of his own!

Sammy Corbett died in France in December 1917 from wounds received in battle, leaving three children including a three-month-old son, Samuel junior. The little boy, who never knew his father, became a 'Ketley character' in his own right. Ironically through his own army service during the second Word War Sammy junior had his own brief moment of fame!

Jacker, who survived the horrors of the war, returned to his native home and a new life. It's not clear how it happened, perhaps Jacker made a call on his old army pal's widow to pay his respects, but whatever it was he became Jane (Jinny) Corbett's second husband and little Sammy's new dad. The well-known Ketley couple had seven children of their own, six girls and a boy, in addition to the three Corbett siblings.

A Ketley Mon

A letter written in France in early January 1919 by Jacker Rigby has survived to reveal a little of the mood and thought processes of a British 'Tommy' at the front during the 'Great War'. Written in pencil the words are fading and the transcript is verbatim:

'No. 200366 L/Corp. J. Rigby 4th Battalion K S L I 'C' Company B E F France January tenth 1919.

Dear Mother, Just a few lines in answer to your kind and welcome letter which I received quite safe. This is the first letter that I have wrote to you for eight weeks but I should have wrote to you before but I had no time as I have got a bad finger and that stopped me writing to you, and dear mother I shall be glad when the time comes that I can come home again for good and then we will have a good time of it, and tell the old chap I hope he had a good time of it. I hope that things are going alright as I may be at home by the time you have received this, let us hope so. If you see E. Jones tell him I am very sorry that I have not written to him but you can tell him the reason that I have not written to him. And you can tell Tom Davies that I hope that he got fourteen days at Salop for 'blabbing' on the Mores. I may tell you that I have written to the Trench Works and I am not going to beg. So now I will close by sending my best love to all at home, from your loving son,

Jack'.

The letter is complete with a battered official army envelope addressed to Red Lake, Ketley. Some of the words are badly faded and there is an obvious family rapport and innuendo that is difficult for outsiders to grasp.

Over eight million souls perished in this war and a staggering twenty-one million suffered through horrific injuries. People said it should never be repeated and the decades of the 1920s and 1930s were approached with an air of unrealised optimism. Modern historians, with the benefit of hindsight, question how the world allowed the Nazi menace to plunge Europe, and eventually the world, into another global bloodbath? In spite of the warning prophecies of such esteemed men as Ketley's Samuel Parkes Camden, there were many that believed Herr Hitler was nothing more than a committed patriot.

When war was declared on that early September day in 1939 Ketley men were once again, as my grandmother was fond of saying, 'not backward in coming forward'. Ketley Brook men Percy and Billy Foulkes followed in the footsteps of their own kinfolk.

Born at 6 Malthouse Row in Ketley Brook, the sons of George William and Elizabeth Foulkes were inseparable as boys. Percy was the elder by two years and the architect of all their scraps and scrapes. At six foot three inches tall Billy was naturally affable, extremely tough and something of a nature boy. It was said that he could catch rabbits before he could read and write. Their father was a nephew of a famous footballing goalkeeper known as 'Fatty Foulkes' who had allegedly played for England, and family members still claim that they are related to another famous footballer, Billy Foulkes of Manchester United's 'Busby Babes'. One thing is clear, all the Foulkes men are described as having, 'hands like shovels', an obvious asset if you want to be a goalkeeper!

Percy followed his dad into the Artillery, and Billy, at nineteen, joined the county regiment, The Kings Shropshire Light Infantry.

Percy had left for France a few weeks before Billy, landing on the continent to join up with the British Expeditionary Force. He died at Caen. Bill found himself in Singapore. Overrun, outnumbered and occupied by the invading Japanese, the British Army which was now out of ammunition, surrendered. He later revealed to a mate that he never even fired his gun.

Despised for what their captors regarded as cowardice and dishonour the soldiers were force-marched to Burma and the dreaded 'Railway of Death'.

The treatment and conditions that these wretched men and women were forced to endure has been well chronicled and I feel that no purpose would be served to elaborate further, other than to remind us all that thousands of souls perished in what must have seemed to them to be Dante's version of Hell.

Years later, in moments of melancholy and too much drink, Billy would let slip details of the lengths men were driven to, hunting and killing wild pigs with crude weapons and starving men reduced to eating the raw meat like wild animals.

Also on one rare occasion, when he was working as a navvy, he removed his shirt due to the heat, exposing the marks and scars of many beatings and floggings. His hardened friends and co-workers pretended not to notice in embarrassed respect for Billy's privacy.

Billy had been released four extremely long years after his capture, and when his friends and family learnt he was due to arrive at Wellington railway station in 1945, they turned out en-mass to give him a good old-fashioned Ketley Brook homecoming.

As the most welcomed train in six war-torn years pulled into the little station men in the uniforms of all the services poured out onto the station platform amid clouds of steam and cheering crowds. Anxious eyes from the Foulkes party scanned the platform for the familiar tall frame of their 'Billy'. The train pulled out of the station and onwards to Shrewsbury with no sign of Billy Foulkes. 'Something must have gone wrong! We've misread the telegraph'. These and other, more worrying thoughts, were left unspoken as the Foulkes party began their short journey back to the Brook. Sister Mary was the first to spot him. Sitting in the family home wistfully staring out of the window she saw what she describes as, "a great big 'Aussie' bush hat pass by the window with the familiar features of my big brother beneath it." "Mam, our Bill's here," she shouted to Elizabeth Foulkes, who had been sitting silently in her fireside chair worrying

A Ketley Mon

whether she still had one son or none? The gaunt thin frame of Billy Foulkes entered number six in Malthouse Row with the cheerful words; "Where's our kidder".

The chilling realisation that Billy was unaware that his best friend and brother had been killed in Caen, France in the August of 1941 dawned on mother and daughter. Too distraught to tell him after all he had gone through they sent him down the Row to another sister who broke the news to a broken-hearted Billy.

The death camps couldn't finish the hardened Ketley man but this news probably hurt him more than any physical pain. As far as Billy was concerned nothing could hurt him anymore, and from that moment on he drifted into a lifestyle of poaching, heavy drinking and violence. Because of his behaviour he constantly fell foul of the local Oakengates and Wellington police, and he NEVER came quietly. The few policemen that knew him intimately, such as the local bobby, Fred Oak, and his relief, Bill Preston, had no trouble with Billy, but others despised the belligerent poacher.

One night half a dozen cops, following a run-in earlier with some of their colleagues, ambushed Billy when he staggered out of his favourite Wellington pub, The Lamb. They jumped him in the dark and beat him with truncheons and their helmets (a formidable if unlikely weapon), but the man who had survived the Jungle and the Japanese just laughed at them!

When I was a boy growing up in Ketley, Billy held legendary status, and from those days to the present I have never heard an unkind word spoken about him.

A few years before he died Billy married and settled down briefly to a life of domesticity in the Sandbrook Estate, Ketley. The marriage, perhaps predictably, failed, and the nature boy returned to his spiritual home, swapping his comfortable Sandbrook council house for a draughty caravan in the south end of Ketley Dingle. Sadly, perhaps mercifully, the tortured soul of William Foulkes departed this world on the 19th of August 1962. He was forty-two years old.

Officially he died in hospital of cancer. Others who were closer to him say he had every disease known to man, picked up during his imprisonment. These rumours only added to Bill's legendary status. My personal theory is that he died years before, on the day he found out that he had lost his best pal and brother, Percy.

Another remarkable Ketley family was the proud holders of what must be a record. Benjamin Spragg lived with his wife Margaret and family at number ten Victoria Avenue. Ben had six sons all fighting for the honour of their country.

The boys were all professionals, joining the services before the outbreak of hostilities. Eli, the eldest, was a Sergeant in the army, as was Will, who served with 'The Terriers' (Territorial Army). Charles Edward Haigh Spragg known simply as 'Korky' and Gerald Spragg were in the Kings Shropshire's. Jack and Eric Spragg were serving with Royal Air Force. Three of the brothers were military boxing champions, as was their nephew Dennis Spragg some years later when, inspired by his uncles' exploits, he joined the Welsh Guards Regiment and became a career soldier himself. The story does not end there. Mr and Mrs Spragg senior had a daughter, Molly, who had joined the A T S during the war and was married to a Jack Price who was in the Black Watch Regiment, also fighting abroad.

To cap it all, Betty, Jack Spragg's wife was also in uniform, she was a nurse at Market Drayton Hospital. Amazingly they all survived! Gerald is the only one surviving from the Record-breaking "fighting Spraggs' of Ketley. He is well into his eighties and now lives in Yorkshire.

The diminutive son of First World War victim Samuel Corbett, Sammy junior followed in his dad's footsteps by joining up with the Kings Shropshire Light Infantry in 1938. Never having been outside the boundaries of Ketley, Sammy junior found himself in what he regarded as foreign parts for the first time when he was posted to Speke Barracks in Liverpool!

The five foot tall Sammy still retains an infectious sense of humour and an 'up for anything' attitude, which is just as well in view of what was heading his way back in 1940!

During the grave days of that year London suffered a terrifying blitz. What is known today as one of those 'and finally', stories appeared in the national newspapers. The tale concerned a young Himalayan bear from one of the London zoos. The bear cub had been made an orphan and was now homeless.

A certain Captain Wycherly, who happened to be Private Corbett's 'Officer', recognised a brilliant public relations opportunity for his Company.

He contacted the powers that be and brought 'Billy the Bear' to Merseyside to be trained as a Company mascot. Billy was still a youngster but was well over six foot tall when reared up on his hind legs. The belligerent bear took a dislike to everyone with whom he came into contact, except little Sammy. Spotting their bond immediately the Captain installed the title of 'Bear Trainer and Company Mascot Keeper' on a bemused Sammy. It was amazing how the pair got on, maybe Sammy's childlike innocence and size connected with the bears psyche, immediately creating an instant compatibility. The army milked the situation for all it could, photos appeared in local newspapers and army periodicals of Sammy and the bear in various situations; bear and soldier in tin hats standing to attention, soldier and bear at machine gun practice and mock wrestling. Billy was growing bigger every day and the artful Sam spotted areas of exploitation.

He convinced the quartermaster that Billy would only eat prime meat and that bottled beer was good for Billy's constitution. Bear and man ate best steak and many a night ended up sleeping off a drunken binge.

There was a down side of course. One night whilst entertaining a local lass at the camp cinema, Sammy at the height of his passion, was interrupted by a message which appeared on the screen " BEAR TAMER COME QUICKLY – BEAR LOOSE". Sammy had to leave the girl in mid-passion to return to help round up 'the absent without leave' Billy.

The Company was posted to Dorset in preparation for going overseas and, naturally, Billy was posted too. The Captain told Sammy that he could stay with Billy for as long as he wanted to because bear and man had bonded so well. Sammy began to have pangs of conscience as one by one his mates were being sent to the front. Torn between his love for Billy and his sense of duty he requested a posting overseas. Reluctantly Captain Wycherly agreed and Sammy was placed on the list. Returning to camp from his draft leave Sammy had a terrible shock. Billy the bear was dead! Probably pining for his trainer, Billy had broken loose one night and went looking for his pal, Sammy. A soldier sleeping under canvas drew the bear's attention and he mauled the unfortunate man, who, Sammy told me, had died later from his wounds. Billy was hunted down and shot. The army had him buried in a deep pit in a local forest.

Sammy Corbett and Billy The Bear. It was amazing how the pair got on, maybe Sammy's childlike innocence and size connected with the bears psyche, immediately creating an instant compatibility.
(Picture loaned by Sammy Corbett)

Private Sammy Corbett was distraught at this news and it was with a heavy heart that he shipped out soon after to join the fighting in North Africa.

Within a few months at the front Private Samuel Corbett was a prisoner of war of the German Army, having been captured at Crete. During his incarceration the little soldier often passed the time relating tales of 'Billy the Bear' to the amusement of his fellow prisoners.

Upon release at the war's end he returned to Liverpool for a short time, but eventually returned to the place of his birth, where he still lives today. Mention Billy and the little man's eyes moisten, "I loved that bear" Sammy tearfully confessed to me.

At the outbreak of war the non-combatant citizens of Ketley were determined to do their bit for the war effort. As in the Great War comfort funds and food parcels for the captured and wounded were set up.

William Henry Lane, a former Flying Corps officer, was one of the first businessmen to contact the War Department with the offer to make light munitions at his engineering factory in Ketley. The site of the factory is better known as the Glory Hole today, even though its modern name is 'Trio'.

Local policeman Fred Oak, who had served in the Coldstream Guards for seven years in the 1920s, had long since passed the status of 'reserve', now busied himself with organising the Special Wartime Constabulary and co-ordinating air raid drills. Prominent residents Billy Upton and Isiah Jones, both local councillors, were among a patriotic group of Ketley men that immediately volunteered to join the Special Constabulary. Ketley also had it's own Home Guard unit and air raid Warden. In the early days of the war time was spent perfecting the air raid drill at the school. With headmaster Mr Dunkey supervising and the official Air Raid Warden Mr Mancell keeping score, their efforts were rewarded. The record time for a complete evacuation of pupils and staff from the school to the relative safety of the old Ketley Canal site 600 yards away, was two and a half minutes.

Percy Dunkey organised the children, boys especially, to 'dig for victory'. "Bring your forks in tomorrow boys", was a familiar order from the headmaster. Allotments at Red Lake and parts of the recently re-aquired playing fields were turned into vegetable patches. The war also brought some positive changes in the form of welfare for the children, a free milk scheme and the opening of the school canteen in February 1940 was a blessing to some. It is recorded that 199 pupils received free dinners, a welcomed first for some of the poorer children.

During this time a German bomber plane discarded or lost one of its deadly packages over the Dawley Road area of Wellington. This was the closest that Ketley got to the war. Exploding on the borders of Ketley in a field at Lawley the casualties consisted of a couple of sheep, some rabbits and a family of field mice!

A Ketley Mon

Ketley Special Constabulary in 1943. The rear row includes Isaiah Jones, Reece Phillips and T Price. On the middle row are Harry Whitingham, B Lewis, Percy Wood, J Whitingham and 'Onions', while on the front row are Fred Oak, Sergeant Barkley, Superintendent Withington, Bevan William Upton and Bert Harris.
(Wellington Journal and Shrewsbury News - courtesy Shropshire Star)

In 1942 an American fighter training squadron were posted to Atcham, the airfild near Shrewsbury.

The squadron used single seater Republic Thunderbolts, which became a familiar sight buzzing around the Shropshire sky, mock dog-fighting while practising their manoeuvres. Several local boys, including Allan Parton, John Doley, Bobby Austin and eyewitness, Arthur Ball swear the following is true. The drone of a plane's engine attracted the attention of the young Arthur, who at that time was living with his family at Ketley Offices, on the main road a few yards from the entrance to Ketley Brook. His best recollection was that it was in the late August or early September time, but he has no idea of the year. In his words, "the plane was really low and I thought it was going to land as it swooped towards the Brook. One of the wings clipped the electricity pylon in the Brook and the plane dove into the front edge of the council tip".

The other witnesses were among a group of local youths who all swear that they saw the aftermath. They say that the plane was mostly buried in the soft ground and that armed police and military personnel, complete with barking dogs, quickly secured and isolated the scene for the investigation into the crash.

A grisly rumour of the time, now grown into local folklore, relates the tale that the pilot's body still remains in the former council tip ground, never having being recovered because of the depth it was buried.

To be fair, there are conflicting stories about the alleged incident. Other witnesses claim the story is myth, one man claims there was a crash in the Brook, but it involved a Spitfire and the pilot survived, and others say the crash was between two American Republic planes mock dog-fighting over the Rock!

Joe Collier, Secretary of the 'Wartime Recovery Group' based at High Ercall, Shropshire did shed some light on the mystery when he informed me that the group had received other reports of the Ketley crash but has no firm evidence to support the stories. Reports of planes crashing in the general area of Ketley are recorded. The dog-fighting Republics over the Rock, and incidents of pilots bailing out at Hartshill near Oakengates at nearby Hadley are two examples.

We may never know the truth of the Ketley Brook 'crash'. I would expect the local Coroners office to have details of any death within its area, but without a date it's difficult to research.

It is possible that a body was not recovered from the alleged 'crash', site, there have been several examples since the war years, including the following. A wartime crash site was discovered in a rural area of west Shropshire few years ago. Part of a plane's wreckage was found in a wood and the body of a Polish pilot recove red, identified and suitably laid to rest.

The American commander of the Atcham Camp, Colonel Miller, who now lives in England, confirms that literally dozens of accidents were recorded during that time and that many were fatal. He has no personal recollection of a Ketley accident but could not rule out the possibility of a fatal crash in the area. The whole incident will probably remain a mystery unless more information comes to light.

Eager to help the war effort, local groups were formed to help in any way that they could. Unfortunately, a petty dispute arose between two worthy charitable causes originating in Ketley. Accusations of misuse of funds furthering political careers and poison-pen letters flew across the floors at open meetings of both groups.

'The 'Ketley Playing Field Comfort Fund' led by Chairman Jimmy Wormstone and Secretary Billy Upton was the older by a few months. 'The 'Ketley Welcome Home Fund', chaired by a Mr W Foy of Red Lake, was equally sincere and committed to the cause of bringing comfort to the service men and women of Ketley. Seven hundred postal orders worth twelve shillings and six pence (62.5p) had been sent to serving men and women over a sixteen month period by the Playing Fields group. Foy's Welcome Home fund had raised over three houndred pounds through various functions. Politics apart, both groups produced a creditable effort.

A unique 'Ketley Stay at home holidays' and annual carnival, complete with carnival queen, was organised by the Playing Fields committee and proved to be a huge hit with the public, raising hundreds of much needed pounds for the comfort fund.

A slightly less conventional method arranged to boost funds was a Rabbit Pie supper held at the Mount Zion Church schoolroom one March evening in 1945.

Mrs F Mottershaw, trustee of the Ketley Playing Fields, donated twenty rabbits, which were made into pies by the ladies of the committee.

A mock auction followed the supper and, with Billy Upton and Jimmy Houlston as auctioneers, the sum of £10 was raised for the cause.

I'm certain that not many Ketley folk, or outsiders for that matter, would believe that a Nazi flag once fluttered over the little town of Ketley, but it did! On a sunny summer Saturday in 1946 Ketley Playing fields were officially re-opened, and the Victory Queen, fourteen year old Beryl Mitton, was crowned.

The event was proceeded by a procession of the local children through the parish, proudly headed by the Wrekin Shamrocks prise-winning Jazz Band. The band had developed during the war and was the brainchild of Mrs Ada Thompson of 4 Victoria Avenue in Ketley. Her daughter, Margaret, and son Alf were the leading lights of the troupe that was made up of practically half the residents of the Avenue.

The committee used the occasion to welcome back the men and women from Ketley that served in the war. The Victory Queen had been chosen by votes cast by the children and the attendants included a little girl, also from Victoria Avenue, whose name was Hilda Rigby. She was the youngest daughter of Jinny and Jacker Rigby. The pretty little girl with the permanent smile was destined to become a local political champion of her beloved Ketley. Little did the young woman who twirled the Shamrock's baton, and the girl proudly attending the 'Queen', know that one-day they would both hold high office in local politics! As Margaret Chappell and Hilda Rhodes, they would both hold the distinction of Chair of the future Wrekin District Council.

And the Nazi flag? Among the many ex-servicemen attending the celebrations was local man Eric Poppett, who, at the capitulation of the German armed forces, found himself in Berlin. The Swastika had been 'captured' by Eric and placed on display as a trophy of war in the marquee where the service men and women were treated to a free tea. The symbol of evil was the centre of attention to everyone present, especially children.

Thank God that the Second World War, horrific as it was, had fewer casualties than the Great War for the little town. There were more civilians killed and murdered through the bombing campaigns and the utter hell of the 'final solution', but this was no 'trench war' with the 'lions led by donkeys' mentality.

Nevertheless, to the bereaved a lost loved one has no numerical importance. Among the eight officially listed dead in the Wrekin Roll of Honour was the son of one of Ketley's oldest and most prominent families. Archie Green had been the postmaster at Ketley for just over twenty years, having taken over from his father William in the early 1900s. His only child, Frank William, was in line to inherit the family business at the shop opposite the Ketley School, where the younger Green had attended. As an accomplished student he had gained a place at the Wellington High School for boys where he developed an interest in the relatively new field of wireless operation. Joining the Royal Air Force at the outbreak of hostilities he became a wireless operator and air gunner. Well-respected by his comrades and about to take his Sergeants exams he was tragically killed in a road accident, 'somewhere in the United Kingdom' (as the military phrased it at the time).

The funeral held in December 1940 drew a large local crowd for the popular young man. Six airmen in dress uniforms bore the coffin, draped with the Union Flag, from the gates of the little Parish Church in Red Lake led by the choir, whose master was Archie Green, the father of the deceased. The cross bearers of St Mary's solemnly and slowly preceded the coffin and the Reverend Davies conducted the service, paying tribute to 'Frank's excellent capabilities' and the pride he had for his hometown.

When reflecting on the casualties of wars we tend to restrict ourselves to those killed in battle. It's a sad fact that more perish through so called mundane causes such as domestic and road accidents, but even sadder were the appalling rise in suicides. It is a subject I had not pondered on before my research, but I came across many entries in the local war papers of tragic suicides, all over the County, including Ketley. Propaganda, fear and the loss of loved ones pushed many to the brink. As an example, the normally reserved residents of Sinclair Gardens in Ketley Town actually built a series of trenches all over the nearby pit mound in fear of the dreaded Hun invading Ketley! The project did have its use though; it became a great play area for the local youngsters!

GHOSTS OF KETLEY BROOK

A walk down Ketley Brook today is a sad occasion for any Ketley born person.

The natural stream that gives the place its name still flows, its origins high up in the Wrekin's hill. The spot, where as a child I first fished for Sticklebacks, now bears the modern-day malaise of a discarded shopping trolley and a sofa with the stuffing hanging out. Smashed glass, scraps of paper and unmentionable items exist in the litter-strewn underpass. The whole area has a feeling of depression and squalor, which is a far cry from the halcyon days of its past when it was know as 'the heart of Ketley'.

The old place names of Malthouse Row, Spring Grove and Ketley Brook Camp, together with Farmers Shop, are long gone, existing only in the memories of the dwindling numbers of former residents and locals.

Situated in roughly the centre of the old community is the remaining Duke of Sutherland cottage that bears silent witness to the colourful past of the place that was originally known as 'Bayleybrook'.

Ketley Brook has always suffered from a bad press and an undeserved reputation, mainly due to a massive influx of workers in the late 1700s. Prior to this, Ketley and Ketley Brook in particular, were fairly quiet and peaceable. Suddenly, invaded by rough navvies and tough iron and coal men, the previously calm hamlet exploded into a scene of almost constant disputes, fights and criminal behaviour.

Ketley quickly gained a reputation as a violent and barbarous place with Ketley Brook, situated as it was in a hollow, becoming synonymous with crime and anti-social behaviour. In the early part of the 19th Century it was said that 'venturing into darkest Ketley Brook by respectable citizens was a perilous thing to do'. A full circle has been turned. Only a few brave souls or strangers would risk walking through the foreboding present underpass at night, even though there are built-in lights!

In the earlier days a policeman named Barber vowed to change all that. High Constable Barber, who was based at Wellington, could be described as the 'Wyatt Earpe' of his time, pre-dating the real Wyatt by nearly sixty years.

As we have read in previous pages, felony and feuding between miners and Irish navvies in particular was rife, and it was an almost daily occurrence to have the Yeomanry Cavalry called into action to quell breaches of the peace in Wellington and Ketley.

Barber, who was the man who helped beat the rioting miners in the 'Cinderloo Riots', made the proud boast that a man would be able to leave a gold watch nailed to a tree in the Brook without fear of it being stolen by the time he had finished.

By the middle of the century peace reigned and the Barber boast fulfilled. Local Brook resident and poet, Samuel T. Morgan penned a poem celebrating the taming of the Brook and the peace gained by Barber. The piece is produced as written;

A QUIET WEEKEND IN KETLEY BROOK

I wonder what's the reason we have such a holy calm,
Resting over Ketley Brook like a soothing charm'
Every day's a Sunday, every hour a bliss,
Oh it's many a long day since the old Brook was like this.

The passers hardly know it; they stop, enquire and look,
They do not seem to realise that this is Ketley Brook.
So peaceful and reposing, contented, charming still,
They would not believe their senses, if it were not for the hill.

Yes there's the hill of cinders, the Horseshoe Inn complete,
The grassy bank, the daisies white, the bungalows so neat.
The castle grand, the famous stores, the rustic porch of green,
But where's the band of music and where's the King and Queen?

Yes the King has left his castle, his old ancestral home,
The Queen alas is absent from the palace and the throne.
Oh Barber, Barber, Barber since you came upon the scene,
You've took the charm from Ketley Brook, and now you've ta'en the Queen!

Samuel T. Morgan

Mainly because of those rough days Ketley was well policed by a series of locally based Bobbies. An early police house was complete with a lock-up at 104 Potters Bank. This house was where law and order was dispensed in the Ketley area well into the late 1930s. Following a spell as a farmhouse it is now the residence of Mr and Mrs Trevor Williams. The building is full of character, and Trevor explained to me that the small lock-up cell was removed to extend what is now the kitchen.

The best remembered and most respected of the Ketley policemen of the twentieth century was Fred Oak, who had arrived in Ketley in 1934. The Brook's reputation had changed little from the last century and the new constable needed to be equal to the task. The thirty-year-old Exeter-born Fred was a former Coldstream Guardsman who had served the colours for seven years. Whilst serving in a troubled China during the 1920s Fred became seriously ill with pneumonia and was not expected to live by his comrades. A rough wooden coffin was made and placed under his cot in anticipation of his death. Waking up with a need for the chamber pot, Fred reached down and under the bed discovered his crude casket. The realisation that everyone had given up on him filled Fred with a fresh resolve to get well, which of course he did.

A few weeks before his discharge from the army in 1929 he had decided to follow his brother into the constabulary. Sitting alone in his barracks room he pondered his future. Determined not to return to his own county he opened up a map of Great Britain and, closing his eyes, he stabbed a pencil into the map, piercing the section on Shropshire. Luckily for Ketley, his application to join the Shropshire Constabulary was accepted, and Fred Oak arrived later that year to what would eventually become his spiritual home.

A regular Saturday shopper in Wellington's Square was smitten with the six-foot tall handsome officer who looked dashing in his police uniform. The admirer was Gertrude Purcell from Cow Wood in Red Lake and one of eight sisters. She married Frederick Richard Oak at Wellington Parish Church on 28th May1934.

Fred, who was another to gain status as an honorary Ketley man, was a familiar figure over three decades of policing the town. Described by many as the 'quintessential village bobby', he was respected by law-abiding residents and rogues alike.

Many a Ketley lad, including yours truly, was surprised, when committing some minor misdemeanour, by the imposing figure of Fred out on patrol on his regulation police bike. He had an uncanny knack of turning up at those times when you were scrumping apples or throwing stones, and his threat to 'tell your dad', and his promise to 'have you put away', had more weight than any corporal punishment. Fred knew his patch and its residents better than the lines on the face he shaved every day. He was a familiar and frequent visitor to the Brook, serving summonses and executing non-payment warrants, but there was a mutual respect between the rogues and poachers and the ex-guardsman, particularly between the other ex-soldiers like Billy Foulkes. Fred was successful because he had that vital ingredient essential to all good coppers – 'common sense'.

A distasteful incident that happened just after the war had a profound effect on the Oak family. A bus driver travelling to Oakengates one day was having problems with some drunken soldiers. The driver pulled up at P.C. Oak's police house, which was then in central Ketley, next to the Allied Ironfounders factory. The driver of the bus asked Fred to throw the troublesome men off his bus.

Unfortunately Fred got a beating and several vicious kicks, causing permanent damage to a kidney, which had to be removed a few years later. Bad health dogged the rest of Fred's career. Very few locals of that time knew that he turned down the chance of promotion to Sergeant and the chance of a desk job. Reluctant to disrupt his children's education Fred chose to remain a constable in the place that had by now, become his adopted home.

William (Bunty) Hall.
(Picture loaned by Billy Hall)

William (Billy) Foukes pictured outside the Queens Head public house around 1950. *(Picture loaned by Lenny Corbett)*

A couple of stories illustrate the mutual respect between policeman and parishioners. During Fred's hospitalisation for the kidney operation Gertie, with two children to care for, was forced to go out and work. In those days when an officer was off 'sick' his pay was greatly reduced causing an obvious hardship. The local Ketley Brook poachers soon got to hear of their old adversary's situation, and pheasants, rabbits and other game mysteriously began to appear on the police house's doorstep.

Fred had been sympathetic to the needs of the poorer people of the Brook, and often turned a blind eye to their poaching, and now they were paying him back! Fred's daughter Dianne is in no doubt that the Brook poachers were the family's benefactors.

Fred Oak, in common with the majority of rank and file police officers of that time was of a working class background, and those ties go deep! During the late 1940s and early 1950s the Oak family planned their holidays around the delivery schedule of a lorry driver from the adjacent Allied factory.

The driver was primed to alert Fred Oak whenever he had a delivery in Fred's home county of Devon. The idea was to hitch a lift down to Exeter to visit his relatives.

Fred, because of his damaged kidney, always sat up front with his driver pal while Gertie and the children, together with their suitcases, found whatever space there was in the back of the lorry. Daughter Dianne says, "those trips were a nightmare sometimes, especially when it was raining and we had to shelter under oily smelly tarpaulins. But at least we HAD a holiday, most of my school friends never got further than Ketley Sands"!

Retiring in 1959 with failing health and a poor pension Fred was forced to get a job at the local Ironworks as a security officer. He died six years later and is buried in a lovely sheltered spot at Red Lake cemetery beside his beloved Gertie.

When I visited the grave to verify some facts, a nearby grave brought back more fond memory of Fred.

Dennis Gordon Jones of Beveley had been two years younger than me and my best mate when we were teenagers. For his sixteenth birthday Dennis had received a brand new 250cc motorbike and we decided to try it out immediately, regardless of licences or insurance. Knowing that PC Oak patrolled the main road and had an uncanny knack of appearing at the most unexpected times, we headed for an area of scrubland known locally as 'the bricklehole'. This strangely named area of Beveley was fairly isolated, with only a few cottages. We were roaring up and down the lane when the booming voice of Fed Oak broke even the bike's throaty sound "What are you two buggers up to?"

We nearly wet ourselves with fear! After a monumental dressing down, Fred made us push the motorbike all the way back to Dennis's home, with the usual threat of being 'put away'. There was no need for summonses. Mrs Jones locked the 'bike up until Dennis obtained the relevant documents. I realise now that Fred was the epitome of a classic village bobby, he knew his patch better than anyone and had that sixth sense knack of being in the right place at the right time. That knack, coupled with common sense gave, Fed Oak the 'edge' that kept the Ketley Bobby one step ahead of us all. Dennis passed away on the 19th April 1979 at the very young age of thirty-five.

During his latter years, Fred and Gertie were a familiar sight strolling around the parish, the ramrod-straight, immaculately turned out Fred with his diminutively built partner, drawing the comment from one Ketley Brook wag, "look at 'em, Lord and Lady bloody Ketley!" The police house was bought by the factory for use as offices and Fred's carefully planned and much-loved garden is now a car park.

The Ketley Brook of Fred Oak's policing era was full of characters, with gypsy 'Coddy' Walker and his wife candidates for the oddest.

No one knew where Coddy and his missus came from, or what his real first name was. They were believed to be of gypsy or travelling stock. The travellers were proving to be so much a problem that the largest landowners, brothers Harry and John Palin of the Rock, employed men, including Jack Moore from the Brook, to collect a weekly rent from the caravan squatters.

Most of the inhabitants of Ketley Brook were poor working class folk scraping a living as best they could, either by 'tick' (buy now pay later), or pawn. But Coddy, either by bizarre choice or circumstance, was so far down the social chain that he was living in a tunnel under the main Wellington to Oakengates road. Most travellers lived a peaceful existence alongside the house dwellers.

Some, like 'Mush' Shevlin for example, evolved from wandering nomad to static caravan in the Brook to house owner in central Ketley! Coddy's main problem was that he didn't mix with the friendly Brook people.

Hermit-like he lived in his dank, dark shelter with Liza, his partner and his old donkey Charlie. The couple survived by collecting 'tat' which is stuff that everybody else would throw out.

Presumably the bits of metal would go for scrap and the rags and other rubbish for fuel. The tunnel, which is about eight-foot in height, is believed to have originated in the late 18th or early 19th Century and leads from the Brook to the foundry on the other side of the road, a good 200 yards. My best guess is that it was used to haul sand from a long since exhausted sand hole on the Brook side of the road. In the mid 1930s an Inspector for the National Society for the Prevention of Cruelty to Children received an anonymous letter about a man and woman living in a cave in Ketley Brook. The Inspector visited, saw there were no children, and passed the matter on to the Sanitation department. There was a lot of tut tutting and talk of a social disgrace whereby people had to live in caves in the modern age, and before anything could be done, Coddy, wife and donkey suddenly gained an

Pictured outside the tunnel in 1999 is 'Cowboy' Chris Clare.
(Terry Lowe)

The Moore family gathering with Jack, Edwin, Percy and Tom behind Edna, Nancy and Jim.
(Picture loaned by the Moore Family)

old caravan which they moved into in the Brook. Nobody knows what happened to Coddy and Liza. One day they just disappeared, never to be seen again.

Their legacy was a children's rhyme sung to the tune 'happy birthday'; "Coddy Walker sells fish, threehalfpence a dish, don't buy it don't try it, it stinks in the dish."

Hard as it is to believe that people living in the so-called welfare state of the 1930s existed in little more than a cave, it's even harder to imagine it happening thirty years later! But it did! In one of the harshest winters for years two men, who had been 'kicked out' of their respective Victoria Avenue homes, lived in Coddy's old home for about three months. Christopher (Cowboy) Clare and Bertie Guy found themselves homeless in December 1962.

Both men were unemployed and made their living like Coddy before them, 'tatting' for scrap or anything else they could find. Familiar with the area they headed straight for the tunnel in the Brook. They rigged up a makeshift tent from bits of canvas they found, and burned wood and surface coal for warmth. The 'cave dwellers' survived for about four months, relying on handouts from friends and the odd hot meal from Chris's mother, Mary, when his dad Alf was at work.

A Ketley Mon

I was disappointed that I could not discover more about Coddy and his cave dwelling existence, but the few surviving locals I spoke to say he just seemed to be there for years and then suddenly vanished when the authorities began poking around. There were, not surprisingly, no details on the census or voters registers about Coddy or his wife; they lived in an age when it was easier to be 'anonymous'.

A rare poem or monologue entitled, 'The Ketley Ass' by Samuel T Morgan, Ketley Brook's resident poet, must have been influenced by the couple's antics. I would like to believe that the humorous verses were a tribute to Coddy, his wife and their donkey.

THE KETLEY ASS

'It's a sad, sad tale of a poor owd donkey. There lay the owd, owd donkey, one Easter mornin' fine, on a bonk of grass lay that owd, owd ass in the sun at dinnertime. His age, I couldner tell yer, not to be up to the mark, but I guess they found him in the mud outside of Noah's ark.

The motors passed him swiftly the waggonettes more slow, on bicycles and on foot they went but the owd ass couldner go. They all were pleasure seeking as he shook his yead and sighed, if I conner go up the Wrekin then I'll commit suicide!

Then he rolled himself reet over and he walloped off the wall; he shook the Brook's foundations and he mesmerised us all. The owd ass was in earnest, I've never seen the such, but he ended theer his long career with just a drop too much.

They sent for 'Reades elixir', they sent for Beecham's pills and Mother Seagles syrup and all that stuff that kills. They telephoned to London, they telegraphed to France; they did everything they could to give that ass a chance.

They called a noted Doctor who drove up in his cab, he shook his eyeglass from his nose and said, 'the ass is very bad'. He ordered best Scotch Whiskey to give it hot and strong, for what would move the missus, would drive an ass along.

But yo'conner turn a donkey when once it's made up it's mind, cos' he inner gonner change it for anybody yo' can find! So, he wouldner take that whiskey, no not a single glass, so he died a good example of a staunch teetotal ass!

Now he's gone to the land of carrots, where donkey's are well-fed, they only work on Sundays and eat Hovis currant bread and bran and mashed potatoes and stabled in sweet hay, and sing the 'Donkey Serenade' at a concert every day.

Now there's going to be a monument at the top of Ketley Brook, with a wreath of donkey thistles, reet handsome it'll look. And every passer-by will read the inscript right and plain of how a dear owd donkey died just theer and Charlie was his name.

And there's going to be a record of all the thrilling tones to immortalise the music of the asses final groans. They'll play it every Sunday and charge thripince for a fee and you'll hear that owd ass die again exact at half past three.

Now the missus had a vision in the middle of the neet of owd Charlie cummin up the stairs in the middle of the night, and he laid his owd cowed nose against the pillow on the bed, and then unto the missus the owd ass sadly said;

'How can you face your Charlie, your dear owd faithful moke, how could you send my body to that stinking knacker bloke? How could you send my owd bones to be ground up in the mill? Three days to go, three neets to cum, your ass will haunt you still.

You should have shown your a Charlie little better luck than to sell him to that knacker bloke for artificial muck. But I'll turn-up in your turnips your tatters and yer grain and in one way or another you will have your ass again.

Now, I'll get these verses printed then if I have the time, I'll pack my bag and sail away to Brazil or the Argentine, so I must catch the fust train to tek me to the sea for on horse and foot and the donkey's ghost they'll all be after me.

[Monologue by S.T. Morgan poet and artist. Circa 1900].

Just after the First World War the Ketley Cinderhill, a huge mountain of slag, dominated the skyline around the Sinclair works and the Dingle. Locally famous, it was featured in a rare postcard of the time. Jack Moore from the Brook could spend all day chasing the gypsies on and around the Cinderhill so that he could collect their rent. Jack and Polly Moore raised seven children in the Brook, twin girls and five boys.

Son James (Jim) Moore was born in 1912 in the Brook and he never lost his Ketley 'twang'. The small sprightly man, whom I met when he was eighty-six, still enjoyed his garden and long walks, especially around his old stamping ground of Ketley.

I felt an immediate bond at our first meeting. His opening gambit was, *"I'm very proud to be a Ketley 'mon', I'm proud of my birthplace and the folks that cum from theer. Some people say the Brook was full of rogues, but it wonner, they looked after their families fust and their neighbours next, yo could go in and out of anybody's house and if they had food and yo did'ner they'd share it with yer. If they'd got no money cummin' in they'd go out poaching, but they wouldner steal from one another, if I could put it this way, the family always cum fust."*

Jim's first job was at Groom's Yard, Wellington, where he worked as a labourer. He met and courted fourteen-year old Dorothy Robinson who hailed from the Ladycroft area of Wellington, and they remained devoted to each other to the day that Jim passed on. The happy and contented couple had settled in nearby Hadley some years ago. They were the classic 'Darby and Joan' couple.

In 1930 Jim had left his Grooms Yard labourer's job for his dream post as a lamplighter with the local Gas Company in Wellington.

The solitude and peace of walking the streets in and around the town, lighting or extinguishing the streetlights, suited the quietly introverted young man to a 'T'. Dorothy, who was an active member of the Union Free Church at Constitution Hill, Wellington, introduced the young Jim to the joys of the activities there. Besides singing, amateur dramatics and craft hobbies, the fellowship was a great character builder. The experience helped to broaden young Ketley 'mon' minds.

Dorothy also introduced Jim to the 'toffs' sport of tennis; the couple played weekly at a privately owned court in Queen Street. The rough and tough crowd in the Brook would have ragged him unmercifully if they had found out, so only his best mate, William 'Bunty' Hall, knew of his relatively young girlfriend and new lifestyle.

Neighbour Bunty and Jim were the same age and were when they were growing up. Bunty lived with his sister, Lizzie Deakin, and her husband Charlie in the house next door to the Moore's in Ketley Brook.

Bunty was a typical fun-loving young man of that time, full of enthusiasm and optimism for the future, and a popular figure among his mates.

To the rear of Sinclairs Ironworks is a man made pool that had been used by the foundry as a natural outlet for the water used in the process of forging and casting, since the first foundry had been erected. Known locally as Parker's Pool, a name inherited from an early occupant of the small cottage at the poolside. The pool's deep, dirty and cold waters are a magnet for fishermen and youngsters. Parents of generations of Ketley kids had been warning their offspring about the dangers of playing at the pool. Mothers told the tale of 'Ginny Greenteeth';

A water witch that lived in the pool's deep and dangerous waters, Ginny reputedly had black skin and slimy green teeth, and would wait patiently in her watery 'garden' for any child to enter the water for a swim. The witch then would swim round and round, faster and faster, creating a whirlpool that would drag the victim down to her clutches. This particular horror story ends with the child being devoured by the water witch. Naturally the tale had the opposite reaction; the thrill of danger was a bigger draw than the unlikely prospect of ending up as Ginny's lunch. Many old Ketley residents still insist that there is a whirlpool within Parkers Pool and to this day the legend exists.

The August of 1933 was a hot and clammy one, so it was natural for the locals, especially the young, to cool off in the waters of the nearby pool. Jim and his brothers, Jack and Percy, called for Bunty on the afternoon of Tuesday 8th August, and the four pals headed off across the Dingle to Parker's pool laughing and teasing each other on that particularly hot summer's day.

A Ketley Mon

When they arrived, half a dozen people were already sitting on the banks or strolling around the pool, including Jack Spragg, and other mates from the Brook.

Jack and Percy Moore, who were non-swimmers, sat on the pool's bank while Bunty and Jim stripped for their swim. As they entered the cooling water on that fateful August day their purpose was to swim from the far side to the bank at the cottage side.

Jim, who remembers every little detail vividly, recalled his conversation with his best mate Bunty. " Think yo' con' manage it Bunt?" With a nod from his friend the pair began swimming to the far side of the pool, a distance of about 200 yards.

Jim, who was the stronger swimmer, quickly made the other side, where he turned and swam back towards the slower Bunty. Turning to swim alongside him Jim queried, "Am yo OK Bunt?" Upon which his pal suddenly disappeared under the water. Instinctively grabbing Bunty's wrist, Jim shouted for help to the others. Nobody did anything immediately believing that the pair were fooling about.

Jack Moore was the first to realise something was amiss, and even though he could not swim he began wading out to his brother, but the sheer drop of the bank prevented him from going further.

By this time Jim, who was exhausted, lost his grip on Bunty's wrist and watched in horror as his boyhood friend slipped down and away. By this time the commotion had attracted a small crowd and a runner had been sent to the Ketley police house some distance away. Several men waded or swam out to the spot where Bunty disappeared, and a couple of them were

Parker's Pool in the early 1950s with the author and his friend from Birmingham, Malcom.
(Terry Lowe collection)

brave enough to dive into the murky waters looking for the missing swimmer, but it was either too deep or too murky.

Sometime later Constable Underhill from Oakengates arrived with dredging hooks and commenced the grim search for the body, which was found in twenty five feet of water, fifteen yards from the pool's edge. A deathly silence fell over the scene as Bunty's lifeless corpse was carried from the pool to the waiting hearse – a works' lorry.

At an inquest opened at the Horseshoes pub in Ketley the following day, a verdict of 'Accidental Drowning' was returned by the jury.

The Coroner, Mr J V T Lander, praised the efforts of James Moore in attempting to save his friend, and he also commented on the lack of barriers to prevent bathers from using the pool and signs warning of the dangers.

Bunty's funeral took place at Ketley Parish Church that Friday with a host of floral tributes and many family and friends present.

Jim Moore carried the burden of his pal's death to his dying day. He was still questioning his own actions on that fateful day. "Could I have done more?" he asked me. I reminded the old man of the Coroner's words at the Inquest, but he just shook his head. Jim's wife Dorothy, who was also a close friend to Bunty had told me; "I was supposed to meet Jim for our regular Tuesday evening tennis game and became worried when he failed to show at the time we arranged. It wasn't like him to be late. When he finally arrived, there was a strange look on his face, I thought he had got the sack from his lamplighters job! When he told me Bunty was dead I nearly fainted with shock. We never played tennis again 'cos it would bring it all back to us."

Thankfully and remarkably Bunty Hall is the only person to have died in Parker's, as far as living memory is concerned. Local folklore has it that a horse and cart sank in the pool in the latter part of the last century, the driver being saved by making an incredible leap to safety!

On the morning of Thursday 9th September 1999 Jim and Dorothy were waiting for a bus outside their Hadley home when Jim was involved in an accident with a car. Jim suffered horrific injuries including several fractured ribs, a broken hip and a serious head injury. Spotting his pet cat straying onto the carriageway and, typically, with no concern for his own safety, Jim followed, and was knocked down by the car. In spite of a week of intensive care at the local Princess Royal Hospital, Jim died from his injuries at 6 pm on Sunday 19th September 1999.

I like to think that Jim has been re-united with his old swimming pal, Bunty and that Bunty has finally eased Jim's conscience.

The latest occupants of the poolside cottage had been Cyril and Doris Poole and their story provides another link to Bunty's demise.

As a young man and long before he moved to the poolside cottage, Cyril had witnessed the drowning incident. Cyril originated from the nearby

A Ketley Mon

town of Wellington and as a young man he worked for the local Gas Company.

Cyril recalled the awful scene of poor Bunty's body being dredged from the pool and the traumatic effect it had upon all present. Cyril, like Jim, remembered every little detail. He had said that the images made a lasting impression on him at the time.

Little did Cyril Poole know at that time that his destiny was to one day occupy the poolside cottage, and stay for over forty years!

Cyril and his wife Doris have spent a working life at the cottage adjacent to the pool. They moved there in September 1954. As probably one of the last of a vanishing breed, their life has been a harsh one.

The smallholding, consisting of a few sheep and chickens, has diminished with the addition of the M54 motorway, which swallowed up a large chunk of their land, but old habits die-hard and standards must be maintained. The ninety-year old World War II veteran, who suffered terrible ill health, could be seen any day working his land. Simply put, 'he knew no other way'. When I visited the spotlessly clean, quaint cottage with its open-hearth fire evoking memories of happier times I felt I was in a time warp. Looking out of the window where a constant stream of motorway traffic passes by day and night brought me rapidly back to reality.

Cyril and Doris recalled the time when all you could see was the fields and trees of what was once Ketley Dingle. Despite being plagued by vandals, thieves and travellers the couple survived and made their living in what some would regard as a tough, lonely environment for fifty-five years.

Cyril passed away in June 1999 leaving the resilient Doris to carry on in the only way she knows how, by continuing the pattern of hard work and dedication set by her partner Cyril.

Although covered in a previous chapter I cannot avoid further mention of Billy Foulkes for, when discussing Ketley Brook, Billy Foulke's name is the first to be recalled. The Dingle was Billy's natural habitat.

Many remember him as I do, pushing his old sit-up-an-beg bike, four ten shotgun and recently caught rabbits hanging from the handlebars and his pair of greyhounds Spider and Bess trotting beside him. His prey had come from either the Dingle or Apley Park, Wellington.

This hard man, who had a fine sense of justice, was the Brook peacekeeper; any trouble and the call would be, "send for Foulky." Stripped to the waist Billy would take on anybody and rarely lost a fight. It may seem primeval today but that was the way it was then. Seldom were grudges borne, and people who fell-out with each other one day were sharing what little they had the next.

Adam, known as 'Ad', and Edith Parton lived next door to the Foulkes family in Malthouse Row. Adam was a brutal bully who treated Edith terribly. He was a petty thief who stole from his employers and from a shop where a relative worked.

His pernicious behaviour constantly landed him in jail. When he was in work he would fly into a rage if food and Woodbines (popular cigarettes of the day) were not waiting for him on the kitchen table when he came hoe from work. Edith, in common with many working class girls during the late 1930s, was married off at a fairly young age to an older man.

The girl's family saw it as shedding a financial burden, basically one less mouth to feed. Heavily pregnant with her first child when they married, the poor girl soon fell into a routine of literally slave labour. Robert, known all his life as Bobby, was born deaf and dumb. The couple went on to have four daughters in a relatively short time.

Edith's prime role in life was to provide, by any means that she could, food, and clothing for the children, and especially, Woodbine cigarettes for her husband. It was simple in those days; the men earned the money and the woman kept the home, and, if she was lucky, her husband may give her a few shillings to supplement her own earnings! On many occasions when Ad came home and the food was served but no cigarettes were present, he would go into a rage, throwing the food, plate and all, into the fireplace. He would then give Edie a good hiding, usually in the shape of a black eye. The only respite was when Ad was in prison. She would pawn his precious best suit of clothes and silk muffler to buy essentials for her children, especially Bobby who was the apple of her eye.

The poorly educated Edith had related to me her version of how her son came to be born without speech and hearing. She had told me that during a night bombing raid on the City of Coventry she had taken refuge under the family table. Fearful that her unborn baby would be affected by the terrible noise she clamped her hands as hard as she could over her ears. She is convinced that this action caused the handicap with which her son was born.

I tried in vain to make the poor woman understand that there was no basis for her theory, and that the rough treatment by her husband was a more probable explanation, but she just shook her head. In spite of her wretched home life Edith's spirit was, and still is, very strong, and her children always came first. She was a good mother, ensuring they were kept healthy and clothed at no little risk to her own health.

While away on one of his prison sentences Edie pawned Ad's clothes and, gathering her children together, caught the morning coach from the Horseshoes to the Five Ways, Birmingham to place Bobby at The Royal School for deaf children. Edith had defied Ad, who cruelly dismissed the child as 'a dummy'. It was bad enough when outsiders called her son 'dummy', but when his own father turned on him she acted.

Bobby had two obsessions as a teenager; he idolised Billy Foulkes, who was one of the few people in the world that had time for the boy, and during his time at the deaf school he became a lifelong 'Teddy Boy'. Billy, who knew Bob would have to face a lifetime of abuse, taught him how to survive in the world.

He took him poaching and taught him how to take care of himself in a fight.

The Teddy Boy fixation came from mixing with boys from the city areas who gave the poor Ketley lad items of Teddy Boy gear, such as brightly coloured drape coats, drainpipe trousers and suede 'brothel creeper' shoes.

Long after the Teddy Boy fad had declined Bob could be seen about the area in one of his many suits, his dark long hair slicked back in a quiff and 'duck's arse' style. In fact Bobby never gave up on the 'Teddy-Boy' style.

Considered as an 'unholy trio' the three Ketley hard men known as, Foulky, (Billy) Jack Spragg and scrap metal merchant 'big Jim' Boardman took the teenage Bob under their collective wing. They taught him all the bad habits of smoking, drinking and fighting and toughened him up.

Jim employed him as a labourer at his Cow Wood Scrapyard where he was in his element, stripped to the waist, cutting up scrapped cars in a cloud of sparks, oblivious to all around him. The job gave the boy self-respect and the work toughened him up. Few called him 'dummy' to his face.

The combination of his appearance, disability and an inherited quick temper inevitably drew Bobby into conflict with the local police, and nights spent in the Wellington police cells were frequent. Like his heroes, these diversions had little or no effect on him. As a local policeman I came across Bobby occasionally and can honestly say I never had a problem. Maybe it was because we knew each other or because I treated him with respect and he me. I never had a cross word with Bob.

Some people I spoke to described Adam Parton as a modern day Robin Hood, only stealing to sustain his families existence and often giving food or cash he had stolen to his hard-up neighbours. According to Eidie the truth is that the money realised from his larceny usually ended up in the tills of local pubs or as clothes on his back! A snazzy dresser he was known as the 'dandy' of the Brook. Dressed in his immaculate suit and best silk 'muffler' he cruised the local pubs at the weekend.

I find it fanciful to compare Ad Parton to the Nottingham legend; as far as I remember I don' recall Robin Hood beating up Maid Marion when he came back to the camp to discover no haunch of venison or jug of ale on the green wood table!

Edith May Parton is eighty-years old and has outlived her husband by twenty-eight years. She has endured absolute poverty in her life.

The lowest point was when she was evicted from her Ketley Brook home that had been condemned as a slum dwelling then quit the house the council placed her and the children in, and returned to squat in her old house! Her children, who were always spotless and well nourished were everything to her, especially her 'Bobby'. The four dutiful daughters ensure she is well looked after, these days, they visit regularly and help with the cleaning and shopping. Edith is still full of spirit told me that she was happiest when Adam was in prison or when she was working on the potato gangs with my late mother and grandmother. The only sadness is the loss of her golden boy, Bobby.

Bobby died aged fifty-six and is buried at Red Lake cemetery. I remember reading about the death of my friend and I had hoped that the lifelong rock and roller had been buried in one of his beloved 'Teddy-Boy' suits but Edie shattered my romantic notion by revealing that all her son's suits are pressed and preserved in her bedroom wardrobe.

True to her working class roots the old lady couldn't bring herself to throw away such a valuable item such as a suit of clothes. It might come in one day! When you've been really poor old habits die hard.

The sole remaining house down the Brook was the scene of a double domestic tragedy concerning a previous Brook resident and his wife. It was here forty-five years ago that a distraught Ben Deakin was found by his son hanging from a beam in a lean-to at the rear of the house. A year previously his gypsy born wife Louisa had passed away in the same house. Born into a Romany family from the Ludlow area of south Shropshire, as Louisa Smith, she had travelled by gypsy caravan all over Shropshire with her father who was a horse dealer. Camped at Ketley Dingle in the early part of the 20th Century the gypsy girl met and fell in love with a Ketley Brook man called Benjamin Henry Deakin.

When the couple announced that they were to marry her family strongly disapproved. In a tribal gesture the Romany ranks closed and put pressure on the girl to marry one of her own kind. She defied her parents and married Ben. According to sixty-five-year old grandson, Eric Deakin. "All hell broke loose. Her family ostracised my grandmother and in the tradition of the gypsy's code they burned her caravan and turned their back on her". Ben and the illiterate Louisa settled down to raise their own family in 14 Ketley Brook.

The house is known by the Deakin clan as 'the White House' because of its colour. Louisa passed away on 5th February 1953 aged sixty-eight. Eric had told me that pit worker Ben was 'beside himself with grief' at the loss of his love and visited her grave at Wellington Cemetery every single day.

The event that finally pushed Ben over the edge came when he was discharged from the pit when he passed the age of seventy-five. On 1st January 1954, eleven months after losing his wife Ben hanged himself at the family home finally re-uniting his soul with his gypsy queens.

The original Duke of Sutherland cottage built in the latter part of the last century has been modernised over the years and has been in the hands of the Hannington family since 1954. It seems fitting that fifty-seven-year-old David Hannington lives and works from the Brook for

The photograph showing a white misty image. Many claim that they could make out a ghostly image of a woman wearing what appears to be a turban head-dress, popular with working women class of the 1940s. David is also convinced that the house is haunted. *(Picture loaned by David Hannington)*

he is yet another one of a dying breed of metal dealers that are indigenous to the Ketley area. In 1997 he decided to replace the fireplace in the main room and in common with many other home improvers David had his daughter Devoone photograph the process. A new fireplace was to be fitted and a series of three pictures were taken of the stripped down open hearth.

When the photographs were developed a white misty image was prominent in one of the snaps. Many claimed that they could make out a ghostly image of a woman wearing what appeared to be a turban head-dress, popular with working women of the 1940s. David is also convinced that the house is haunted. He claims to have felt a presence in the old house and had his suspicions re-enforced one evening when his German Shepherd dog, Zeus showed signs of being disturbed by 'something' in the room where the fireplace was changed. Aware of the double deaths of the Deakin family, Hannington showed the pictures to Ben and Louisa's grandsons. Eric, who is an accomplished amateur photographer, has an open mind concerning the picture with the 'image' and had the camera and film examined at a Birmingham laboratory. The analysis was inconclusive! Clive Deakin, the other grandson that viewed the photo said he could make out an image of a woman wearing a turban similar to the one his grandmother, Louisa Deakin used to wear! I have shown the picture to friends and relatives and three out of five say they can definitely make out a face of some kind.

Of the three pictures, two are very clear in detail and the third does have a cloud of white mist or smoke over the area of the unfitted fireplace.

With a little imagination a face or at least a part of a face and a possible turban can be seen. I remain sceptical and have no reason to doubt Dave Hannington's or the Deakins sincerity, they are people I have know for a long time and among the last I would expect to believe in ghosts.

A final mystery is linked to the Brook's long and colourful history.

On a sunny August day in the early part of the 1980s eighty-year-old George Price from 'Glenferris', Station Road, Ketley, walked out of his front door and was never seen again. Brother-in-law and next door neighbour to the late Ketley grocer, Alf Whittingham, George was well known locally. Dressed in his familiar dapper manner with a jacket and neatly pressed trousers, shirt and tie and the ever-present trilby hat, is how most folk remember him. On the morning he disappeared he was carrying his plastic shopping bag as usual and when he closed his front gate he turned left and walked down Station Road in the direction of Wellington. When he reached the National Tyre depot opposite Sandbrook Estate, a matter of seventy-five-yards, he shouted across to the opposite side of the road to Jack Smart who was leaning on his front garden gate. "How bist Jack, lovely day." Jack swapped pleasantries and commented on the warm summer's weather, then watched the little the old man stride off towards the direction of Ketley Brook. That was the last time any body saw George Price. Within a couple of days the concerned widower's relatives reported George missing to the police and a hunt was commenced, for what the police now believed would be a body. Despite an extensive police search and the dragging of all the local pools, including 'Parkers', the nearest to where he was last seen, no trace of George has ever been found. The popular local theory is that George committed suicide because of the death of his wife some months before. Many believe that he threw himself down one of the giant culverts being installed in the Ketley Brook area for the management of storm waters. It's certainly possible that someone could fall or jump into the concrete castings and not be seen. The work was being pushed along at a rapid pace and where there was an open giant hole one day, was filled in and levelled the next.

Perhaps George Price lies with other lost and restless souls believed to be still earthbound within the Brook's boundaries? We will probably never know!

THE QUEENS HEAD MURDER

If the question in the popular television show 'Family Fortunes' was, "Name a famous Ketley murder"? I guarantee that every Ketley born person watching would leap up and shout at the screen, "The Queens Head"!

Most of the people I have met have heard of the incident but all have different versions of it. Here are the facts.

"The money won't do you any good my lad." Jane Edge's dying words would haunt her killer to the end of his days.

William and Jane Edge took over the Queen's Head public house in Ketley from the retiring landlord William Peake in 1924, quickly becoming popular and accepted by the inhabitants of Ketley Brook who considered the 'Queens' as their pub.

Two years later William died and Mrs Edge became the landlady of the pub, which stood on the old A5 road above the Ketley Brook conurbation. She ran the pub while bringing up her three children, Jack, Bert and Emma.

Early pictures reveal a striking and imposing woman who gradually endeared herself to the regular drinkers at the homely public house. The regulars consisted mainly of Ketley Brook hard men who bore a mutual respect for the warm-hearted woman.

Jane, in turn, had a reputation of her own. She kept good beer and good order in HER house, which is why most of her customers respectfully referred to the portly landlady as 'Mrs Edge'. The 'Queens' gained a reputation for fun and 'having the crack'. 'Crack' has Irish gypsy origins and roughly translated means having a good old gossip. The pub echoed with the laughter and spontaneous singsongs of its customers, who were in the main working class. Instead of walking all the way up or down the Brook road and then back down the main road to get to the pub, people did what they always do in these situations. They found the shortest rout by creating a pathway from the bottom of the Brook up alongside the pub, which was known locally as, 'The slit'.

Sunday lunchtimes were a ritual. Men would begin gathering on the stone wall adjacent to the pub some time before the 12 o'clock opening time. Billy Foulkes, Jack Spragg, Adam Parton and others would enjoy the 'crack' bragging about the mornings poaching or last night's punch-ups.

The late 1940s and early 50s were the glory days for the pub and the traditional Sunday dinner time session, lasting two hours in those days, were the best. Trained musician and local boy Trevor Williams would play the piano for ten bob (fifty pence). Trevor who lived at the old original Police House on Potters Bank had contrasting musical backgrounds.

Learning his skills on the local chapel organ as a tot, the young serviceman when, on leave from the Royal Air Force, was the Mount Zion Chapel organist playing hymns in the morning and lunchtime swing king at the Queens pub.

At about 2.30p.m. On the afternoon of Wednesday 6th September 1950 Elsie Poulter who ran a roadside mobile cafe opposite the pub unwittingly became the last person, apart from her killer, to see Jane Edge alive. She had witnessed the familiar sight of Mrs Edge throwing out crumbs for the birds as she locked up following the lunchtime session, acknowledging her neighbour with a wave of her hand.

At the end of his shift at a local factory Jack Edge routinely called at the pub to see his mother. He had recently married and moved from home, but such was the closeness of the family they saw each other most days and that September in 1950 was no different. Jack was surprised to find the front door locked, it was usually left open in anticipation of him calling, or if it were a pleasant day his mother would be waiting to greet him from her chair in the pubs doorway. Making his way round to the back door he found it closed but unlocked. The second sign of something not being 'quite right' came when his mother's little dog failed to greet him as normal.

Jack discovered his mother slumped in an armchair in the front room with her Pekinese dog lying at her feet. His first thoughts were that his mother's weakening heart had failed her but then he noticed blood about her head. In the bar Jack found the clear signs of a struggle, broken glass on the floor behind the counter, a quantity of blood and the empty till drawer. Now shocked and fearing the worst he hailed a neighbour to fetch the police, who arrived in the shape of the local constable Fred Oak. Fred arrived and quickly assessed the situation sealing the scene for examination by his detective colleagues. He broke the terrible news to Jack that his mother was dead. Jack then had the unenviable task of telling his brother Bert and Sister Emma the tragic news.

Detective Chief Inspector Evans from Wellington was next to arrive with his team and then professor James Webster, Home Office Pathologist was summoned from his Birmingham laboratory. The initial theory was that Mrs Edge had been emerging from the cellar and disturbed a thief rifling the till and in his or her panic had hit the poor woman with a heavy glass pint mug, and slowly that theory developed into fact with the physical evidence found at the scene.

Dougie Osmond the Chief Constable of Shropshire in a press conference held the following morning revealed the post mortem results which amounted to Jane Edge having died as a result of a violent attack. He also informed the press that he had called in 'The Yard' (It was a common practice for provincial police forces in those days to request the Scotland Yard Murder Squad to assist with a murder enquiry). Great fuss was made of the fact that Mr Osmond had also called for assistance from the

A Ketley Mon

The Queens Head public house around 1930 as seen in this view which shows a line up of five luxury buses of the period preparing to leave on an excursion. *(Picture loaned by Ray Phillips)*

Lancashire fingerprint expert, Chief Inspector Campbell, who had fingerprinted 50,000 people resulting in the capture and conviction of Peter Griffiths the Blackburn child killer. Murder Squad Detective, Superintendent William Henry Rudkin and his team arrived twenty-four hours later. An appeal for lunchtime drinkers at the pub brought forth sightings of a man in a brown coat.

The murder shook the town of Ketley and horrified the many friends and customers of the Edge family. Three days after her death hundreds lined the old A5 route of her funeral cortege.

Ironically at the same time as the funeral a routine check of a casual workers hostel at Apley near Wellington was being carried out by local officers. Frank Griffin, a Bolton-born forty-year old married, but separated man, who had quit his job at Joseph Sankey's works at Hadley two days before the murder, returned to his room at the hostel after a dinner time session in a Wellington pub. He was surprised to find the police in his room. A cream coloured shirt that belonged to Griffin which bore signs of a number of minute blood spots, and his Gladstone bag, which contained a large amount of silver coins, were seized.

Jane Edge photographed around 1920.
(Picture loaned by Ray Phillips)

William Edge pictured around 1920.
(Picture loaned by Ray Phillips)

Griffin made a statement to the effect that someone had planted the money in his bag and that the blood was from a slight injury at work. After the police left Griffin told fellow hostel dwellers that he was leaving for Birmingham to find work.

Griffin then disappeared from the Wellington area.

On the afternoon of Sunday 10th September the local policeman at nearby Ironbridge was informed of a stranger at the local Tontine Hotel who was acting suspiciously. P.C. Basil France and another officer went to the Tontine and were told of a man calling himself Jenkins was spending heavily on drink.

France sent a porter to summon Jenkins to the reception area of the Hotel.

When twenty-five minutes had passed without an appearance of the guest the officers went to his room. The occupant of Room five gave his name as Jenkins and took sips from a gin bottle from time to time as the officers questioned him.

Basil France was immediately suspicious when the stranger tried to evade questions about his circumstances.

A Ketley Mon

The astute Basil decided to take a 'shot in the dark' and queried if he had ever been to the Queens Head pub at Ketley and the stranger replied, "Do you mean the pub on the main road? Why do you want to know?" France replied, "I think you know" and 'Jenkins' sitting on the bed with his head in his hands allegedly broke down and said, "It wasn't worth it, she fell down and I hit her with one of the pint mugs. I took about £20 from the till, it wasn't worth it." PC France wrote down the confession and invited Griffin, who had by now revealed his real name, to read and sign it. Shaking uncontrollably Griffin passed out leaving a dramatic line of ink down the page of the officer's notebook. Arrested and taken to Ironbridge police station Griffin was given the opportunity to sober up before further interviews.

Superintendent Rudkin the officer leading the enquiry listened intently while Basil France read the notes in his pocket book, and stared stone-faced as Griffin denied having murdering Mrs Edge saying he had been too drunk to know what he was saying when he confessed to France. Later that evening he was charged with murder.

Appearing at Wellington Police Court the following day, Griffin entered a plea of 'Not Guilty' to the murder of Jane Edge. He was arraigned to the County Assize Court.

During the three-day trial at Shrewsbury Assizes in November Griffins movements prior to and after the murder were revealed and closely cross-examined.

On the morning of the murder he was seen in the Red Lion public house on the Whitchurch Road, Wellington. This was shortly after 2.00p.m. He was then spotted walking between the Cock Hotel Island and the Buck's Head pub near the headquarters of Wellington Town Football Club. He was heading in the direction of Ketley, where the next pub on that route would be The Queens Head.

At about 3.40p.m. a local refuse collector saw a man inside the Queens bar. He assumed it was either Jack or Bert Edge. The next sighting is at 9.50pm the same evening when Griffin enters the bar of the Plough pub, Whitchurch Road, Wellington. The following day Griffin was observed in a Wellington pub buying expensive whiskey when witnesses swear he previously only drank beer. This was the day he was first seen by the police and the shirt and bag seized. The blood on the shirt proved to be of a common type of which the deceased shared with a majority of the population.

A key piece of evidence concerned a suitcase Griffin had left at Bill Perry's house and cycle shop in Park Street Wellington, on the day he disappeared.

When he went to collect the case he paid Mr Perry twenty-five shillings (£1.25) that he owed him. Griffin had asked Perry to change £5 in coins for five pound notes, pouring a large amount of coins from a buff coloured bag similar to one Mrs Edge used.

A most damming statement to Mr and Mrs Perry which Griffin would feebly deny making, was to lead Griffin up the gallows steps; Allegedly he remarked to the Perrys, "You haven't seen me tonight". A total of thirty-nine prosecution witnesses gave evidence including the Pathologist who described nineteen separate injuries to Jane Edge in what would have been a violent struggle in her pub bar. Basil France predictably got a grilling from the defence lawyer, Mr A.J. Long over the 'drunken confession' at the Tontine; he was accused of deliberately getting Griffin drunk in order to obtain a confession.

Every eye in the packed courthouse focused on Frank Griffin as he arose to give evidence in his defence. Dressed in a light brown sports jacket with a white handkerchief in the top pocket a striped tie and grey flannels he looked confident.

Great play was made of the fact that he had suffered memory loss and hallucinations through blackouts caused by a disease contracted in Mexico some years previously.

He told the court about the time fellow hostel dwellers had to calm him down when he was discovered fighting with the foot of his bed. On another occasion they had found him sparring with a tree outside the hostel. He admitted going to the Queens Head pub for a drink on the fateful day where, as the lone customer he drank two pints of bitter served to him by Mrs Edge.

He had asked for a third pint but she had suggested that he come into her kitchen for a cup of tea. As he walked through the bar to the servery area he saw the open till and stole money from it. He claimed that Mrs Edge had seen him take the money and came at him screaming, "What are you doing, robbing me?" After a struggle Griffin claimed he helped Jane to her sitting room and fetched a dishcloth from the kitchen to wipe some blood from her mouth. He claimed he had left the pub unaware the landlady was seriously injured. Griffin conveniently had no recollection of the visit to Bill Perry's cycle shop, and denied taking a string of imitation pearls from the pub. Evidence of the burnt remains of a synthetic nature similar to imitation pearls had been introduced during the trial but was inconclusive regarding identification.

Mr Long concluded that Manslaughter was the appropriate sentence because intent to kill had not been proved.

Mr Justice Cassells summed up, telling the jury that if they find that the defendant was so drunk that he couldn't have formed the intention to kill or inflict grievous bodily harm, and then he would be guilty of 'manslaughter'. However, if they decided Griffin's drunkenness merely meant that he could more readily become violent and was still capable of intending to kill or cause grievous bodily harm then he would be guilty of murder.

Following a two hour deliberation, broken only once for a clarification on a point of law, the jury returned a verdict of 'Guilty of Murder'. Asked if he had anything to say before the sentence, Griffin replied, "I would just like to thank my counsel my Lord, for a superb fight. That is all."

Placing the black cap on his head, Justice Cassells sentenced Frank Griffin to death and he was removed to the death cell at Shrewsbury prison.

The Court of Appeal dismissed his Appeal after Griffin's Counsel had stated that there were no grounds on which an appeal could be argued.

On the winters morning of 4th January 1951 Albert Pierrepoint the Public Executioner and his assistant, Herbert Morris hanged the first man at Shrewsbury Gaol since, the similarly named William Griffiths of Eccleshall Staffordshire in 1923.

A crowd of about forty gathered at the gates of Shrewsbury Gaol including Mrs Edge's sons Jack and Bert and her son in law, Ray Phillips who had been in attendance every day of the three day trial. An unidentified Shrewsbury woman placed a newspaper on the ground at the time of Griffins final farewell to this world, and prayed for the Lord to have mercy on the murderer's soul. Local policeman Bill Preston stood respectfully to attention as a lone prison bell tolled.

The Queens Head murder had a profound effect on the Ketley area at the time, and even today nearly fifty years later people still recall their movements at the time in the same way that President Kennedy's assassination or the Munich air disaster is remembered.

If Griffin was tried today under the present rules of evidence and procedure there is no doubt that he would have been convicted of manslaughter and avoided the gallows, if capital punishment existed.

Almost certainly the damning 'confession' taken in Room five at the Tontine would have not been allowed, and Griffin's medical condition would have had more bearing on the eventual outcome.

There are a couple of footnotes to this case, which I would believe are quite interesting. The first is by way of a spooky coincidence.

As I left the research room in Shrewsbury's Records Centre having just read the newspapers report of Griffin's trial, I bumped into an old friend that I hadn't seen for some years. Wilf Bright is a Ketley lad and a school pal from Sinclair Gardens. Wilf and I had been close during the 1950s and 1960s until we went our separate ways, and ironically we had only met on two or three occasions in thirty-years.

Co-incidentally we both entered law enforcement. He joined the prison service as an electrician warder and I had joined the Shropshire police.

As we stood chatting on the pavement in Shrewsbury about the good old times I mentioned the coincidence of my reading about the famous old

Ketley murder and then immediately meeting someone from those days. Wilf nodded and then told me a gruesome tale. " I dug Griffin up"! Searching for the telltale signs of 'wind-up' in his eyes, I listened, as he continued, "No joke". "A few years ago due to development at the prison the graveyard had to be excavated and the bodies moved to another part of the prison grounds, so I volunteered and dug up a group including Griffin".

Wilf was not kidding and we both commented on the grisly coincidence of our meeting.

Another local legend surrounding the place of Griffin's capture takes the form of a ghost story. Allegedly eerie sounds and lights switching on and off in room number five at the Tontine Hotel, Ironbridge are evidence of the tortured soul of killer Frank Griffin. The current licensee Trisha Gentleman has received dozens of reports of weird noises, taps turning on, bright lights appearing and creaking floorboards.

Ray Phillips, Mrs Edge's son-in-law revealed an experience he had when he visited the hotel with his daughter and her husband. After having eaten a meal they were discussing the murder and arrest in Room five when he swears that suddenly the heavy menu card which had been on the table 'jumped' up a couple of inches from the table landing with a bang. Ray, a committed sceptic cannot explain it.

Room five has now become locally famous as a haunted place and is chosen frequently by volunteers under charity sponsorship. The tales of the ghostly room have drawn visitors from all over the globe eager to experience the ghost of Mrs Edge's killer. I have visited room five at the Tontine but did not experience any ghostly happenings though I confess that there is a distinctly cold spot in the middle of the room. My only regret in this case is the lack of photographs of Griffin. Ray, who had plenty of time to study Griffin every day in court told me that a dummy figure on display in the actual cell at the Old Ironbridge Police Station and museum, is a very close likeness of the killer. Dozens of people I have spoken to about the Queens Head murder are convinced that Griffin was the final person to hang in Shropshire.

Let's put an end to that argument right here!

Griffin was NOT the last man to hang at Shrewsbury, that distinction goes to a twenty-one-year-old Shrewsbury butchers assistant named George (Sailor) Riley who murdered sixty two year old widow Adeline Smith, in her Westlands Road home in the town. Riley was hanged at 8.00a.m.on Thursday 9th February 1961.

THE BEAST OF BROOKHILL CRESCENT

The battering of Jane Edge in 1950 and the bludgeoning of William Bailey in 1812 evoked extensive local revulsion in Ketley, while the Cow Wood pit murders had a widespread effect within the community, but the murder of a twenty-seven-year-old social worker on 5th November 1980 surpassed all human belief.

The incident highlighted the vital need for the various agencies to share confidential information. In the aftermath of this disturbing case the Police, Social Service and Probation Service eventually set up a system for a sharing of intelligence gathered about their respective clients. Edward Samuel Walker was born the son of a works painter and an Irish servant girl in February 1947. The boy was born in a local council house in Wrekin Road, Wellington. His infrequent attendance at the local St Patrick's Catholic Junior School in North Road, Wellington and his inability to settle sealed his early fate. Quickly falling into a life of petty crime he was placed in care at eight years of age. From the age of ten to his final arrest for murder in November 1980 the juvenile delinquent had graduated from Council care, Approved school and Borstal to long term imprisonment. 'Teddy Boy Walker' as he was now known was disliked and feared by most people because of his violence, or despised because of his indecency towards women. At about this the time he had been assessed by some agencies as a 'loner and moody person with a drink problem and a sadistic streak'. His lifestyle when not in custody was one of drinking and petty criminal behaviour.

The only friends he appeared to have were fellow criminals. Those that knew him well say he had never worked since he left school.

A passion for the American singer Elvis Presley became an obsession. Whenever he was in his favourite local pub, the Barley Mow in Wellington town centre he would constantly play Presley songs and this, together with his Teddy boy suits, earned him his nickname. Little did the young moody Walker know that one-day he would earn a more sinister nickname! Teddy Boy Walker was akin to a walking time bomb and nobody in authority picked up on it. His actions on bonfire day 1980day would earn him the chilling title of 'The Beast of Brookhill Crescent.

In 1969 his mother, Adeline, divorced his father Samuel and travelled with her only son to her native Dublin. In November of that year Teddy joined the Irish Defence Forces as a trainee soldier. Two months later he was discharged as 'unsuitable'. Returning to England he married a local girl at Wellington Registry Office and obtained a council flat in Hawkestone Court in the Dothill district of Wellington.

Amazingly, the abused Eileen Walker reconciled with him after a spell in prison by Walker for violently assaulting her. But the reconciliation was short-lived and divorce followed in 1977.

In February 1979 he was sentenced to three years for burglary and assault, and was released seventeen months later. With his wife long gone, his father dead and his mother back in Ireland. Teddy briefly went to live with his sister and her husband at Dee Close, Wellington. After badgering the local housing authority he was allocated a flat at 136 Brookhill Crescent in Ketley where for a brief period he kept a low profile.

Exactly six weeks after his release from prison Teddy opened his door to an attractive young woman who worked for the Shropshire Social Service Department.

An application for supplementary benefit had brought twenty-seven year-old Rachael Mary Edwards of Ellesmere, Shropshire to the door of the dangerous Walker. Rachel's parents were farmers and she was an active member of Nesscliffe Young Farmers Club. She was popular and well liked in the close-knit farming community.

Misfit Walker invited the unsuspecting woman into his sparsely furnished flat persuading her to join him in the bedroom, on the pretext that it was warmer than the living room. Like a predator toying with its prey Teddy even let Rachael go through the charade of completing the official forms before suddenly attacking her.

The unsuspecting young woman was subjected to the most unspeakable sexual acts as well as being raped several times by the sexually frustrated Walker. Rachael's ordeal lasted for hours and a feeble attempt to escape only brought on more abuse from her tormentor. The monster having gone so far decided that he had to kill the woman and his deranged mind formed a plan. 'Kill the woman in the most inhuman way and cop a plea of insanity!'

The cosy council flat had now become the lair of the beast.

Rachael's parents were abroad on holiday that November so when her brother Mark realised that she had not returned home by the following day, he notified the police. As soon as she was reported missing the police began re-tracing her movements using her calls list. Eventually they arrived at 136 Brookhill Crescent, Ketley and the discovery of Rachael's yellow Ford Escort car outside Walker's flat. Upon the discovery of the body a murder enquiry was commenced.

Hardened police officers were sickened by the scene that faced them inside the flat, 'what kind of monster were they looking for?' Edward Walker was quickly arrested at the home of one of his relatives in Wellington and he readily confessed to his vile crimes. Appearing at Stafford Crown Court in July the following year he pleaded 'guilty' to murder and rape and after a twenty-minute hearing he was sentenced to life imprisonment. Mr Justice Pain commented on Walker's extensive criminal record, which he thought was insignificant compared to this appalling case and he made no recommendation for a minimum term of imprisonment. In a rarely taken step the Judge ordered that a copy of Walker's statement would be attached to his file for consideration by any authority considering his release. The Prosecutor, Mr David Smout made reference during the hearing that officers of the Social Security department did not have foreknowledge of client's criminal records, which prompted the agencies concerned to review their procedures in relation to the exchange of confidential information.

This case more than any other helped to establish the setting up of 'At Risk Registers' and indirectly, the sex offender register which should hopefully prevent another 'Beast of Brookhill Crescent' happening again.

Some years ago I saw a television documentary on life-serving prisoners and was sickened at the sight of a sneering Teddy Walker whinging on about the injustice of keeping a man locked up for life. I'm certain the friends and relatives of Rachael Edwards would have shared my disgust at the programme.

Brookhill Crescent does not exist today; the name having been changed to Wedgewood Crescent a few years following the horrific events that took place there on that fateful November day in 1980.

An aerial view of Ketley taken in 1974 showing the Shropshire Star offices to the left of the A5. On the top, left-hand corner of the picture is Brookhill Crescent. *(Courtest Shopshire Star)*

MORE KETLEY CHARACTERS

It is my belief that Ketley should be remembered for it's key role in the Industrial Revolution and all that came out of that period, not least the invention and successful running of the first Inclined Plane in this country. Others will say that the true riches of an area exist within the character of its people and Ketley, like most of the villages and towns in the world has had its fair share of local 'characters'. The thread that binds all my candidates for 'character' status is not their eccentricities or oddness but their pride at being associated with the town of Ketley. In short, each one is a true 'Ketley Mon' or 'Wench'!

By the very nature of its industrial heritage Ketley was bound to be an area where many would earn their living from the iron and scrap metal business. For example, two Ketley boys who were born in the same era to working class parents made trading in scrap metal their forte. Although entirely different in temperament and lifestyle they shared the same gritty determination to succeed.

Robert Baden Austin, known by all as, 'Bobby', was born sixty-eight years ago approximately fifty yards from where he lives today. The front door of 5 Station Road in Ketley opened directly onto the main road and the back door onto an area known as 'Day's Building' and the Old Forge Row.

The 'Mission' building which was reputably a 19th century miner's mission, was adjacent to the Austin household. The collection of buildings owed their existence to the nearby foundry, whose coal-black emissions had, down the years, covered the area with a coating of sooty grime. The only time that the women could do the family washing was when the factory was inactive!

Bobby inherited his unusual middle name from his dad who in turn had been similarly blessed with the hero of Mafeking, Robert Baden Powell's full name.

Robert Baden Powell Austin had arrived in Ketley via Oakengates and not surprisingly, he became a local Scoutmaster. He was also a leading member of the Oakengates branch of the Salvation Army. Dozens of young Ketley youths, including my father, joined the newly formed Scout Troupe. Ketley was considered too small for it's own troop so the boys had to travel to either Oakengates or Wellington for their scouting activities. Bobby was, as he puts it, the 'black sheep' of the area. Refusing to join his father's scout group he displayed an early individualism, which he still possesses today.

Modest Bob admits freely that he is not an educated man. He insists that his lack of education is because his mother, who was widowed early on in her married life, had four children to rear. Skipping school and taking crop picking and labouring jobs when he should have been sitting at his Ketley school desk, was the only way he felt, that he could help his mother.

Two years national service with the Infantry and postings to Somaliland, Mogadishu and Cyprus broadened the young Ketley lad's outlook. In common with most conscripts of the time, Bobby 'did his two and got out'.

A return to his hometown found him, like thousands before him, working in the foundry at Sinclair's as a moulder. It didn't take this former soldier long to realise that the smoke and dirt of the foundry were definitely not for him. Fresh clean air and an independence to roam freely was more to Bobby's liking, so he took a bold step by buying a second hand lorry and in his words "going out on the road tatting for scrap or anything I could make a shilling on".

Today he is a familiar figure in most parts of Shropshire and neighbouring counties through his itinerant dealings.

Bobby's trademarks are his ever-present smile and infectious personality, but more importantly, his honesty and pride at being a 'Ketley Mon' through and through. Bobby still enjoys the thrill of what he refers to as "the odd deal here and there".

I have known Bob all my life and as a child I always believed that he would make a great circus clown. His rotund build and chubby cheeks support my childish image. A recently discovered photograph of him as a small boy disguised as 'Happy', one of the seven dwarfs at an early Ketley Carnival, confirms my childhood image!

Bobby learned what he refers to as, "dealing" skills when he lived down the Brook during the early days of his married life. There were still a few travelling people and gypsies around the Brook at that time and Bobby had a great affinity with his new neighbours and especially their community parties at Christmas time. Generous to a fault they would share food, drink and bon homie with anyone and everyone.

Bobby had mastered how to barter as a kid, a rabbit for a fowl or vice versa, but mixing with the gypsies gave him a unique insight to the art of trading, gypsy style. "I was taught by one of the best" says Bob, "Mush Shevlin, who had a caravan in the Brook, would come and see you and start by asking about a wheel for a car for example, but all the time he's interested in something entirely different. He pulls you in and then suddenly takes you by surprise by asking your price for what he really wants, and very often he got it for a lot less than it's worth".

As if to reinforce what he was saying, the telephone rang several times while I was talking to him and it was clear from the one sided conversations that Bobby was still enjoying 'the deal'. Weirdly one of the calls came from the late Mush Shevlin's son Adolphus who is still carrying on the family business of 'dealing' from his Oakengates home. "He was asking about a pick-up truck, explained Bobby, but I suspect it's 'summut' else he wants, he'll be ringing me back later."

Well passed retirement age, Bob still works, not for the money, but for the pure thrill of getting the best in a deal. So complete is the cloning you could be forgiven for thinking him of gypsy roots.

Completely opposites in appearance, business styles and temperament to Bobby was another Ketley scrap man called Jim Boardman. The 'rough and ready'. James Edward Boardman also spent a virtual lifetime in the scrap metal business.

Born at Ketley Sands Jim went to school in Ketley with contemporaries Billy Foulkes and Jack Spragg. If ever a man was born to be scrapman it was Jim.

He lost the little finger on his left hand fleeing from the watchman at the Ketley scrap heap, which was at the edge of the Ketley Dingle. His co-conspirators, Foulky and Spraggy had convinced the ten year old Jim that the loss of his 'pinkie' was a symbol of true 'hardness'.

Leaving school at thirteen to work in the Ketley foundry he answered the call from his country when he joined the RAF as a driver in 1943.

During his war service Jim met and married an attractive young Welsh ATS girl named Lillian Vaughan and shortly after the war settled down to a life of domesticity. Following demob Jim first worked as a steel-erector and began dabbling in the scrap metal market on the side.

Within a short time he graduated to full time dealing at a site in Cow Wood, Red Lake. Lilly as the anchor took care of the books and paperwork and Jim in his element, provided the muscle.

In the post war era the scrap business boomed. It was dirty, dangerous and hard work but Jim and Lilly successfully raised their kids in an environment of metal being crunched cropped and generally mangled. Conversely it was also a haven for foxes, rare wild plants and other creatures that are rapidly vanishing from our countryside.

The comic character 'Desperate Dan' could have been modelled on James Boardman, except for his language. My father, whom I never heard utter a swear word, and at five foot five was a complete contrast to the big scrapman, was a close friend. They had sat next to each other at Ketley School. My introvert dad helped the slow learner Jim with his lessons and in return he protected my dad from the school bullies. That friendship paid dividends for me when I became a local policeman in the area. Most officers were greeted with gruffness and insults whereas I was welcomed in the traditional friendly Jim manner " of, how the **** are 'yer' young Lowey"? Lilly fed me fairy cakes and cups of tea whilst I inspected the records, subtly distracting me when I encountered missing entries with; " how's your lovely mam Terry luv"?

My everlasting memory of the giant Jim is of him stripped to the waist in all weathers, cursing all and sundry with the foulest language and throwing huge chunks of metal around as if they were balsa wood.

Jim died in 1995 and with him died the last of his breed, a self educated man with a 'work hard- play hard ethic'. In a harsh environment Lilly and Jim had raised a family and retained their pride and dignity. Despite of his rugged looks and gruff exterior James Edward Boardman had a kind heart, he took lots of waifs and strays under his wing, for example he gave Bobby Parton a local deaf and dumb boy work when no one else would. When local people talk about Ketley characters Jim Boardmans name is prominent. I still keep in touch with Jim's widow, Lilly and her famous fairy cakes.

Gordon Robert Hardy, known as Bob is a genuine Ketley-born success. He quotes Jim Boardman as his source of inspiration when he first decided to go into business for himself. "I admired Jim for his work ethic and determination to succeed" Bob had told me.

The son of a Chesterfield miner who came to Ketley for the work in 1935 Bob was born on Broadway Estate in Ketley four years later. Leaving school at fifteen he began an electrical apprenticeship with fellow schoolmate and Ketley boy Allan Parton, at a Wellington electricians firm.

Quitting Robert Jones electricians firm after only a few weeks set a pattern for Bob. A number of casual jobs including stints in motor trade, coal mining, manager at a tile shop and tyre fitting led him eventually to a slightly more stable role as a manager at Dunnings Tiles store in nearby Oakengates. Management gave Bob a taste for power. He married his life partner Joan in 1963 and later began a new venture with elder brother Tony that was to put Gordon Robert Hardy on the first step to becoming a millionaire. The brothers launched their venture in very humble surroundings. A pre-fabricated building on a small piece of land opposite the old Charlton public house in Oakengates was tucked away from the other mainstream businesses of the area but nevertheless became quickly popular with the motoring public of the area. Hard graft and working all hours paid off and within a short time the name, 'Hardy Tyres' was as familiar a name to local motorists as their own.

Normal sibling rivalry apart, the brothers had a good working relationship but Tony decided to branch out on his own and found himself being drawn towards a career in the licenced premises business.

The Hardy family has a strong Ketley link, their father and mother had run the old Seven Stars for several years and both boys have fond memories of the old pub.

Tony; the elder brother by four years had a natural bent for the licence trade so it was a natural progression for him when he became a licensee.

An affable persona disguises the hard-edged business brain possessed by Bob Hardy and expansion of the Hardy Tyre depot was next on the agenda.

Investment in much larger premises in New Street, Oakengates merged into trading in second hand cars. The hard work was beginning to pay off.

Today Bob is able to look back and make jokes about his ill-fated attempt at being a night club entrepreneur.

The appropriately named 'Jubilee Club' was opened by Bob and his partners in the year of the Queen's Jubilee, 1977. Naivety and a lack of preparation brought the twin disappointments of failure and a lighter pocket. Bob transferred his share of the club to his elder brother who, with true entrepreneurial skill turned it into a strip club with the appropriate licences, and a short-lived instant success with the maxim of 'give the people what they want', was guaranteed. Genuinely pleased that his brother had been successful where he had failed, Bob returned to what he did best and began expanding his tyre fitting business with a greater emphasis on motor trading.

With the trappings of success came a designer-built home at Quarry Lane, Red Lake with the obligatory swimming pool. Joan and Bob dreamt of lazy hot days sipping chilled wine in their own back yard, but the dream turned into a nightmare. Towards the end of the 1970s the excavation of the old quarry pit in the rear garden of the home began in earnest.

Brother Tony and other business associates all chipped in with the work. The project soon gained the basic shape and depth, was ready for the grouting process. A days work saw the tiles grouted, but when inspected the following morning, all the tiles were lying at the bottom of the hole and the grout was just a pile of powder.

The initial explanation was a reaction to the grout by the quarry stone, but despite several attempts they were unable to get the tiles to stick. In desperation Bob called in the local council who, after several attempts finally got the tiles to stick. Everybody believed that the grout had an adverse reaction with the tiles. However, a more sinister explanation emerged.

The Hardy's teenager son Simon was the first to experience an unusual incident. Lying in his room one day listening to some music from the 1960s, appropriately, The Searchers 'Every time that you walk in the room', Simon, was dosing with his eyes half closed when he says he became aware of 'something moving' on the landing. "It was a figure in a white shirt pulled up so that it appeared headless, Simon recalled, It seemed to be dancing up and down to the music".

Simon swore that he had not been drinking or taking drugs of any description and that his initial impression was that what he believed he saw was a man.

Bob, who was downstairs at the time, heard his son scream out and said he ran, "like bloody hell up the stairs." When Simon told his father what he had seen Bob's immediate reaction was that an intruder had entered the house. A search failed to reveal anything suspicious.

The noises came next, footsteps, doorknobs turning and little creaks and bangs.

After an experience with the door handle turning without reason Joan decided that she could no longer remain in the family home. She believed it was haunted.

An article in a parish magazine about a man being murdered in Red Lake in the early part of the 19th Century drove an exasperated Bob to call in a local priest to perform an exorcism. Despite this Joan refused to return to the house and Bob sold their 'dream home' to a Hindu family. He had told them of the 'happenings' but they said that they did not believe in ghosts. Strangely or coincidentally a short time after moving to their new home the couple lost a child to the cot death syndrome!

As a sceptic I find it difficult to except the concept of ghosts, but there are a couple of facts that I find intriguing in this tale; The battered body of William Bailey who had been murdered in 1812 was dumped in the Red Lake quarry pit by the killer. That original pit was believed to be in or near the area that became part of Hardy's new swimming pool. Even more chilling is the little-known fact that Bailey's head was removed by the surgeon to be produced in Shrewsbury Assizes at the subsequent trial. Simons vision was, allegedly a headless dancing 'man' in old style white shirt.

Bob and his family now live in a ghost free house in another part of the County. He coyly admits to being a multi millionaire. Money hasn't changed him as far as his humour and character goes; he retains his affable style and has never forgotten his roots. Bob is the quintessential

Bob Hardy's swimming pool at Red Lake.
(Picture loaned by Bob Hardy)

local boy made good who still gets a buzz from assisting son Simon who now runs the family business. In common with Bobby Austin, Bob Hardy cannot resist the thrill of 'the deal'. During my interview his phone also rang frequently.

Brother Tony, born James William Anthony Hardy in Chesterfield arrived in Ketley when he was few months old. After the success of the Jubilee Club the elder Hardy brother decided to settle into the more traditional side of the licensed trade by taking over the Omnibus pub on the old A5 road at Oakengates.

Tony and wife Peggy purchased an imposing 19th Century house at 103 Potters Bank Ketley. Their son, Chris, had bid for the property when it came up for auction eleven years ago. Tony and Peggy were abroad at the time but backed their son's judgement and moved in when they left the Omnibus pub in 1988.

Chris, who had occupied the new home until his parents took up residence told them of strange unexplained noises and smells that he had experienced. They put it down to the fact that the house had been unoccupied for some time.

The old house has a massive cellar, which was once the servant's quarters and kitchen area on a split-level. There is a separate servants entrance and access to the upstairs landing. The 'longroom', which was used as the dining area, conjurers up images of elegant dinner parties and Victorian opulence.

The first step upon moving into the new home was to have it modernised and redecorated. Workmen began to tell tales of persons moving about in the house when nobody else was there, and unexplained feelings of a 'presence' in the building. Tony experienced a pungent musty smell; he described it as "almost like rotten cabbage being cooked." but at the time dismissed it as the natural ambience of the old house.

Peggy swears she felt a 'presence' or something or someone pass by the bathroom one evening when she was in there with her eighteen-month old grandson Darren. Her initial thought was that Tony, who had gone out for the night had returned home for some reason. A check of the house showed it was secure with all doors and windows locked. Tony later confirmed that he had not returned to the house.

When the family converted the house into a bed and breakfast guesthouse reports of residents hearing voices began to filter back to the couple. One guest swore something had lain across his sleeping body waking him up.

A clue to the mysterious happenings came by way of a carpenter who was staying at the home for a few days.

At the breakfast table one morning he commented that he had heard one of his hosts calling their grandson 'Darrie' (Darren) on the servants landing in the middle of the night. Bemused because Darren was not staying with them, and they never used the servants landing when guests are staying, Tony and Peggy were convinced that their house was haunted.

Peggy, who married Tony in 1957 claims she had a psychic experience when she was a child. She says she was sitting by the old fashioned open grate at her home in Hadley when she saw a 'little old lady dressed all in black' who shuffled by her and drifted directly in the flames of the fire. She says she wasn't frightened but when she informed her mother she was told that the description fitted exactly her deceased grandmother.

Surprisingly calm about the ghostly happenings at 103 Potters Bank the Hardy's remain indifferent about 'the presence'. They say they have no fears and grown used to their 'ghost'. In fact they regard it as, 'a friendly guest'.

Cynics will say that a resident ghost may draw curious guests to the B & B thus boosting trade, but the couple says they have never exploited the fact that they have a ghost. Apart from the immediate family and a few guests no one knows of the ghostly stories that are connected with the old house.

Trying to make some sense of the stories I decided to probe the history of the house and it's previous occupiers.

The last resident was a Mr Henry Kendal and his wife, Nellie who had lived there for many years. Henry who had suffered the loss of an arm during World War I service had a sister who came to stay at the house from time to time. She was an artist, scholar and world traveller and normally lived in the Channel Islands.

One night Mrs Kendal who suffered ill health collapsed in her bedroom and the one-armed husband unable to lift his wife called out in vain to his sister, Dorothy by her family name of 'Dorrie'. The connection is self-evident.

Coincidence? I leave you to decide!

Hard-edged businessmen thrown from the same clay of thousands of down to earth Ketley men, Bob and Tony Hardy are among the last people I would have thought believed in such things as ghosts. I don't doubt their sincerity, I just remain sceptical.

The next subject in my list of Ketley characters caused me wonder what the odds would be of two boys from the same small town and similar backgrounds becoming multi-millionaires? And even more remarkable, both still living today more or less in the area where they were born?

Bob Hardy and Joseph Wellings both attended the same Ketley School and are the first to admit they are not well educated.

Joe is another Ketley man who hasn't travelled far from his place of birth. In fact, Joe lives in the exactly same place at Hill Top Farm, Ketley Town. You would guess right away that he was an outdoor man, ruddy coloured cheeks and laid back manner belies Joe's business brain, he's another of those natural born dealers like Bobby Austin and Bob Hardy.

William and Mable Wellings settled at Hill Top in 1939 having moved from Cantlop, Berrington near Shrewsbury. Over the next thirty years farmer Bill became well known throughout the country as a fine breeder of horses through his excellent stud stock. As boys the Wellings and their friends including a Ketley Town lad called Alan Ball taught themselves to ride the ponies that roamed their Ketley meadows. Usually riding bareback, young Alan was a natural and upon leaving school the diminutive boy sought a career in the world of horse racing. Leaving school and home at fifteen he became an apprentice jockey under another famous local man, Sir Gordon Richards. Forty years later his talent for breaking horses is still in demand in his present home of Marlborough.

Sadly the stud part of the business faded when Bill died in 1969. The decision to build a new motorway gobbled up the precious grazing land in the area that the Wellings family used to graze their horses and thus brought an end to a much loved business. From stud horses to heavy plant may seem an unusual step but the Wellings brothers, Joe and elder brother Jeff made it a very successful one. Who would have thought of painting a refuse skip an unlikely pink colour turning the 'Big Pink Skip' project into a thriving local concern? The Wellings brothers that's who!

Joe's rugged outdoor appearance and laid back style masks his natural charm and cultured communication skills. I caught up with him when he had just returned from Malaysia and already he was planning his next buying trip to India.

He continues a family tradition with a keen interest in horses and a healthy respect for the countryside. Joe recognised early that to survive you must adapt in a changing world. Millionaire Joe is another fiercely proud Ketley 'mon'. Not as outwardly dynamic as the Hardy boys, but Joe shares the shrewdness and business acumen necessary to survive in the cut-throat world of heavy plant machines.

'Champion Eater',
Jack Duggan with drinking partner **Colin Sandford** on a local hosteller at Oakengates.
(Picture loaned by Janet Williams)

I never knew Jack Duggan from Red Lake but I wish I had. He was one of those eccentric persons that every village or town in the country seems to have. Jack was born just before the First World War in Ketley he remained there all his life. A lifetime bachelor, Jack was well known and welcomed wherever he went. Amazingly, when you consider his lifestyle, Jack lived to the ripe old age of eighty-three. He died in a Dawley based nursing home some years ago.

He originally lived in an old cottage in Red Lake but moved out to a caravan in the same area during his later years. Described by his friend Jerry O'Sulivan as "A great character who was about sixteen stone in weight and five foot eight inches tall".

One of his trademarks was his flamboyant hats. Sometimes it was a straw boater , and other times it was a genuine leather cowboy hat that was given to him by Jerry. "It made him look like 'Hoss' from the western series Bonanza", Jerry had remarked to me.

Jack had worked as a groundsman for the Ministry of the Environment at Cosford aerodrome, Shropshire. A big eater as a child his appetite grew with his size until one day he graduated to the human equivalent to a waste disposal unit!

Pub licensees all around the area welcomed Jack with open arms knowing their profits would be up that day.

At a normal sitting Jack would consume twenty to thirty sandwiches, a dozen packets of crisps and perhaps a full card of pork scratchings washed down with ten or twelve pints of ale.

Claiming a world record (unofficial) of 400 sandwiches and nineteen pints of beer at one sitting, Jack was in his competitive prime between the ages of forty and sixty, until health reasons forced him to cut down when he retired at sixty-five.

One of his more gluttonous feats was to finish off an unbelievable thirty-six portions of fish and chips with peas in an Oakengates fish and chips shop during an eating dual with another man. The challenger was hospitalised!

In an interview for the Telford Journal fifteen years ago he had told the reporter that he had never been in the Guinness Book of Records. Jack stated that he did write to them once and they confirmed that they listed eating and drinking records separately but had never received a claim for a joint record. Officers from the air base attempted to entice him into appearing on television but he declined.

The stories of Jack Duggan's eating and drinking feats range from the ridiculous to the sublime. One man swore that he witnessed Jack eat a complete jar of pickled eggs and then swallow the vinegar, another swore he saw him eat live frogs! Drinking partner Colin Stanford described Duggan perfectly; "Jack was a big man with a bigger appetite".

Sadly, characters like Jack Duggan don't exist today. He lived in a time when everybody seemed to be a 'larger than life' character in their own right but I would say without fear of contradiction that few were as flamboyant or as big a draw as big Jack, especially when he sat to down eat and drink his way to another record!

In an era when every boy wanted to be a train driver when he left school, John Henry Parton dreamt of being a barber! Born in the rural village of Longden-on-Tern in the early 1920s and educated at Hadley school.

At fourteen he became an apprentice to local Wellington barber, Bert Richards. Two years after war was declared he was called up and joined the Royal Engineers serving to the duration.

In 1946 he came to Ketley for the first time. He rented a shop in a building known as 'The Mission' which was a prime spot being surrounded by dozens of houses. His family had cleaned and fitted the shop out whilst he went through the process of demobilisation.

Situated on the main Ketley road, there was a pub twenty-five yards away, the HorseShoes and the areas largest local employer, Sinclair's on the other side of the road. As he contemplated his new venture he wondered if the ten bob (50p) a week rent he was to pay owner/shopkeeper Jack Dunning, was really worth it?

A teenager with natural wavy hair was the new barber's first customer. Introducing himself as 'Jack' Parton, John Henry started snipping away. When the cut was finished the young Dennis Spragg from nearby Victoria Avenue looked approvingly into the mirror, his naturally wavy hair looked good so he and handed over a tanner for the cut (2.5p), and walked out of the shop. One of Dennis's mates asked him where he'd had his hair cut and Dennis replied, "Jack the barbers" and unwittingly Dennis created a local legend.

Jack the barber, besides cutting men's hair (unisex hairdressers were twenty-five years away), sold the traditional barbers accessories, the popular Brylcream hair dressing, razors, combs and what were known then as 'French letters' or 'Johnnies' (condoms). Bob Hardy had told me a tale typical of the 1950s. Bob and his best mate Bud Allen were all set for a Friday-night jaunt to Stafford and needed some 'protection'. They tossed a coin and Bob lost. Entering the barber's shop the young Bob panicked at the site of a woman in the shop and stuttered the first words that came into his head. Back on the pavement and heading for the bus stop, Bud said, "Did you get 'em"? Bob sheepishly pulled out-a tin opener! "Great, that'll be handy if we come across a chastity belt", Bud observed!

Because of re-development of the area Jack the barber had to move in 1958. He took over the shop that cycling champion Ernie Clement had used in central Ketley which was also a good spot being next to Alf Whittingham's grocery shop and directly opposite the Aga works factory. One day Noel Jones, another Ketley character, who was one of two

A Ketley Mon

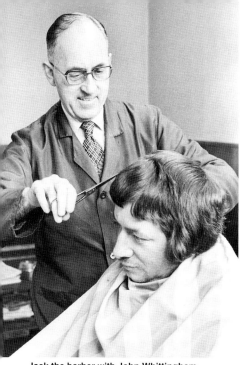

Jack the barber with John Whittingham.
(Picture loaned by John Henry Parton)

John's father, Alf Whittingham, outside his Ketley shop around 1950.
(Picture loaned by John Whittingham)

brothers who lived together in Hadley Road area of Ketley rushed into Jack's shop Claiming 'sanctuary', he told Jack that his brother Harry was threatening to 'kill' him following a sibling squabble over something and nothing.

Noel, another character, was known as the 'Ketley Spiv' due to his habit of hanging around street corners. He spent the majority of his time conducting the traffic at the Seven Stars crossroads.

The slothful Noel would slouch, cigarette drooping from his lips, directing vehicles left or right at the tricky crossroads with the minimum effort. Just a nod of the head to the left or right was the only clue the motorist would receive.

Noel sat in the barber's shop all day, reading the papers and swapping gossip with the customers. When Jack closed the shop that night Noel was last man out.

On a cold December day in 1964 Jack was preparing to administer short back and sides to a shop full of customers when someone rushed in to announce that the Seven Stars was about to go under the demolitions hammer. Never one to miss an opportunity Jack rallies a group of waiting lads and leads them the hundred yards to the doomed pub. Jack knew that the stylish red leather bench seats from the pub's lounge were to become fuel for the bonfire so he had promised the brewery that he would find them a good home.

A Ketley Mon

Motorists gaped as the boys hauled the seats back to Jack the barbers shop. Little did one of the bench carriers know that twenty-three years later he would take over from Jack when he retired? (I guess that the 'laying-out door ended up on the bonfire).

As Jack prepared to shut up the shop that Friday night in 1985 a final glance round the unusually empty shop brought a tear to his eye. The newspapers and magazines were all in their racks and the last carpet of hair had been swept from the linoleum floor. Locking up for the last time he stepped out onto the pavement to wait for his lift home. A breathless Percy Spreckley from Sandbrook, Ketley rushed up and said; "Am I too late Jack?" "No Perce, come inside." Jack replied, "You'll be the last of the day."

Despite retirement a dwindling number of old customers still call at Jack's Wellington home for their short back and sides. Although not born in Ketley Jack the Barber is an adopted son, he is the epitome of what a perfect barber should be, a good listener and a non-gossip. Whatever secrets were told, and there must have been lots, remain firmly locked inside the head of the man known forever as 'Jack the Barber'.

Twenty-three years after he helped carry the benches from the old Seven Stars, Ketley Brook born Alan Butmara picked up the scissors in the small Ketley barber's shop to continue the local connection. Alan was born in the old army huts in Ketley Brook and is still shearing the heads of the local residents in Jack's old shop, thus carrying on the tradition started in 1946 by the old master himself, 'Jack the Barber'.

Not all my characters are colourful. Sometimes when the 'little man' takes on the 'big man' a different kind of character is needed. The following story is an example of that:

A small family ran furnace in the Wrens Nest area of Ketley town was one of the last of the small businesses of its type. Originating from the middle of the nineteenth century the great grandson of the founder who was born in the Wrens Nest still lives in the area. He is seventy-seven year old World War Two spitfire pilot Harry Pritchard and he is proud of the achievements of his ancestors and remarkably calm about the circumstances that brought about the downfall of the business.

Harry's great grandfather, John Pritchard established the furnace and John's son, Richard Pritchard, worked it together with other family members until 1937 when Richard died. The Pritchard's claim to fame was the unique metallurgical formula that enabled them to produce castings that were more durable than their powerful rivals were producing. The steel rolling mills of Haybridge, Trench and the Lilleshall Company relied on cast iron guides that acted as buffers against the white-hot steel. The basic idea was that the guides would take all the wear when coming into contact with the precious steel. The same applied to the 'slippers' or braking system on the horse and cart transport of the day.

As a young man. Harry had worked with his grandfather in the family business and the intention was for him to own and run it when the old man died.

Harry's father, who had been badly wounded in the First World War, was not fit for the demanding work so Harry was to carry the bulk of the workload. Then the Second World War came and Harry joined the Royal Air Force serving with distinction mostly abroad, returned home in 1946. He was devastated to discover that his beloved foundry had been stripped down to the basic brick construction.

The boilers and the engine which once were the heart and soul of the little furnace were gone, taken either by thieves or officially for the war effort, either way they were now re-cycled into munitions or other objects vital to the country.

Undaunted and driven by 100 years of tradition Harry painstakingly re-built the business as well as the machinery. Assisted by his now frail father he began supplying the magic formula guides to the local steel mills again. An article entitled; 'The Furnace in the Orchard' prompted an old Wellington Grammar School pal, Gordon Lowe to write to Harry. Gordon originally from Oakengates represented an American owned company called 'British Driver Harris' who had a rolling mill in Cheadle Heath near Manchester. The firm was interested in the claim that Harry's furnace was producing guides that had a working life of an unbelievable 24,000 hours whereas other suppliers guides lasted only 2,000 hours. The Manchester based company was rolling a nickel and chrome mixed product that was extremely resilient thus reducing the lifespan of the normal guides and the little Ketley-based furnace were the answer to their prayers. Unfortunately due to a combination of property development and metal licensing restrictions Pritchard's contract came to an end and Harry found it impossible to work the furnace at a profit.

He was mystified when no one made an offer for the family secret, but resigned to his fate he obtained a position as an assembly supervisor at the nearby Allied Iron works. Harry has no regrets about the past; he is one of the few people that I have met who would more or less do the same again if he had to relive his life.

He is reminded of his legacy every night when he puts his head on the pillow in the custom-built bungalow less than a 100 yards from where he was born. It is the one tangible reminder of better days, paid for by money earned from the furnace in the orchard.

The Ketley Town junior school now occupies the site of the old furnace and Harry breached the generation gap a few years ago when he visited the school to talk the local children all about the 'Furnace in the Orchard' and his family's proud heritage. The secret will die with him!

Most of the women in the Ketley area worked at one time or another with the potato picking gangs that had origins in the war years. Some, like

Edie Parton found comfort and solace within the band of happy sisters. "It was like having a great big extended family" she had told me.

Encouraged by the government during the Second World War non-combatants volunteered to work on the land to aid the war effort. The women of this country rose to the challenge and the vast 'land army' was born. The practice of crop gathering by woman 'gangs' carried on well into the late 1950s especially in little towns and villages such as Ketley.

The name of local woman Lucy Thomas became synonymous with the gangs raised in the Ketley area. She was larger than life in both character and appearance.

She dwarfed her mild mannered husband Ralph. Lucy definitely wore the trousers! Lucy as 'ganger' (leader of the group) organised the workforce with my granny as second in command. The largely built Lucy drove the workforce through her physical presence and her booming voice. My gran, Emma Lowe, who held the respect of the women was the only member of the gang of whom Lucy looked up to. The partnership of rough tough authority and elder stateswoman worked perfectly.

In those dark days whole families boarded rickety old trucks or omnibuses to be driven to countryside farms. Mothers brought along kids of all ages especially during the school holidays, to help the women in any way that they could.

The work was seasonal and depending on the time of year the gang would be pea picking, potato picking, or beet hoeing. Occasionally there was a break from the norm when fruit picking and hop gathering was the agenda for the day.

Every pair of hands, no matter how small, was put to use in this time of great shortage. The entire community benefited. The farmers gained a highly motivated and relatively cheap workforce and the women earned extra, much-needed cash. And then there were the perks of free produce that sometimes meant the difference between feeding the family or not.

Emma Lowe and co-worker Beatie in the Ketley fields around 1950. The work was seasonal and depending on the time of year the gang could be picking peas, potato picking, or beet hoeing.
(Terry Lowe)

It was tough backbreaking work but the camaraderie among the workers was unbreakable. Any farm worker foolish enough to tangle with a member of the gang would find themselves totally outnumbered.

Upon arrival at the field 'lengths', usually six of Lucy's ample strides were marked out with elderberry stick markers. Hessien potato sacks would be cut up to make crude aprons to gather the crop while the smallest children were secured in rough crèche's made out of bales of hay. Other infants who were not old enough for picking were detailed to look after the ' little uns'. The pay was meagre so everybody was on the fiddle; the larger potatoes, or 'roasters' as they were called, were put to one side and stashed away in voluminous shopping bags or the bottoms of babies prams.

The countryside provided a whole new word to us children. The older ones were sent on egg hunts, collecting free-range chicken and duck eggs. Rabbits bought from the farm workers for a shilling each (5 pence) eked out the family budget. I remember that during the 'Davy Crockett' fad of the early 1950s many in Ketley, including my brothers and I, sported hand made 'coon caps', complete with a white bobtail, skilfully fashioned from rabbit skins. My mother could skin and gut a rabbit in 5 minutes flat! My main memory of this process is the smell of the guts and blood, and the lifeless cold eyes of the poor creature. To this day I have not eaten rabbit. A roast rabbit often made the difference between eating a meal or not in those days, but disease put the break on rabbit as a popular meal.

It was the practice of many of the farms during and just after the war to employ Prisoners of War who were distinctively dressed in work clothes that had a yellow circle on the jacket and yellow stripe down the leg of their trousers. The local hamlet of Sheriffhales, near Shifnal, was the site of an Italian prisoners of war camp, a fact that I would be personally grateful for!

When I was old enough to understand, my mother told me the story of how I nearly suffered under the wheels of a farm tractor when she was working on the potato gangs. Apparently I was about three or four at the time and left to my own devices as the women worked. I was playing between the potato rows blissfully unaware that the tractor was bearing down on me with its deadly spikes flicking the spuds out of the furrows. The tractor driver, who was looking back at the machinery at the time, was unaware of my presence.

The women workers, backs bent in labour were also ignorant to the danger but a mother's instinct made my mom look up to see where I was.

A scream and a shout prompted a yellow-striped figure to leave his work and make the few yards dash to snatch me from what would have been certain death.

I vaguely remember the incident. My memory is of a warm summer's day, I recall a great deal of fuss being made of me, and I distinctly remember a man in a jacket with a big yellow circle on it. There is no doubt

Mrs E France sitting outside her Ketley Offices home. Behind her are the Days Buildings. *(Picture loaned by Mary France)*

'Bowling for a Pig' on the Horseshoes back field sees Jacker Rigby with the cup. Behind are Albert Guy, Jimmy Moore and landlord Lamsdell. *(Picture loaned by Amy Parry)*

that this unknown former enemy saved my life and I have no means of thanking him for that.

Lucy and Ralph had two sons The first born, Ralph, suffered a terrible accident whilst at school in Ketley. In the 1930s the school railings were topped off with jagged spikes and twelve-year-old Ralph climbed the railings one day on a schoolboy dare. Poised atop the unfortunate Ralph slipped and pierced his rectum causing a horrific wound, which later turned gangrenous killing the poor boy. This was the second accident involving the railings in the space of a few years. The first tragic incident occurred around 1930 when another Ketley boy called Jack Williams lost the sight of an eye through falling on a spike whilst climbing the gates for a dare. The authorities had the deadly spikes cut off but the original ironwork railings remain at the school. Lucy's second born son, Kenneth was what my granny called, 'a hellbat', or in other words, a scallywag. If there were any mischief afoot Ken Thomas would be at the bottom of it.

Any 'punch-ups' and Ken Thomas would be in the thick of it. Lucy and her troublesome offspring suffered a love-hate relationship. She would die for him one day or half kill him the next. A tearful Lucy once confessed to Emma of throwing a bread knife at Ken one particularly fraught night, missing his head by inches!

On one occasion in the potato fields Ken refused to do any work, clips around the head from Lucy failed to get any response so she warned him that if he wouldn't work he could walk back to Ketley. At the end of the day she stuck to her word and refused the fifteen-year-old access to the bus. A final flurry of foul language from Ken sealed his fate. Despite the other women's pleas she ordered the bus driver to 'carry on' and Ken began walking the eight miles back home. After dropping all the workers off Lucy walked into her house in central Ketley to find Ken tucking into a doorstep sandwich of bread and jam, he had hitched a lift with a motorist a few minutes into his walk.

Ken Thomas is a Ketley character in his own right, a notorious self-confessed womaniser with a tinderbox temper.

Possessing a vocabulary of the foulest language and no respecter of gender he can be found almost any day in either the local betting shop or the Horseshoes pub loudly expressing his opinions. Ken claims that he doesn't realise he is swearing because it is so natural to him but his loud distinctive voice has made many a maiden blush.

His rough and gruff manner belies a certain charm and 'The Ketley Stallion', a nickname he is still known by today, boasts that he has had more women than Errol Flynn! He claims to have lost his virginity at thirteen with local girl Lizzie Gregory. Enticing the slightly elder Lizzie and one of his pals, into his mother's hen house to do the deed. Amid the unromantic surrounding of feathers and chicken muck the passion of the occasion made Ken forget to close the pen and the inevitable happened; Lucy spent hours rounding up her flock.

A good hiding from Lucy for letting all her fowl escape marked the event but had no effect on Ken whatsoever. That's Ken for you, larger than life! Still living in a flat at Ketley the ageing Casanova revealed his great love for his mother and how much he misses her, his blue eyes moistened when he spoke of her, unfortunately his choice of words are unprintable!

It would be remiss of me not to mention Ketley School's very own 'lollypop lady', Dolly Amoss. Dolly served as such for over twenty-seven years. Unpaid at first, she became a familiar figure and traffic guardian to generations of Ketley children and parents.

When the formidable Dolly strode out into the middle of the A5 with her 'Stop-Children' sign speeding motorists screeched to a halt. Her glare froze many a curse on the lips of a late for work driver. She certainly was a fearful sight to travellers, but a loving protector of her tiny charges. One unkind wag described Dolly's face when she stared down motorists as akin to 'a bulldog chewing a wasp'. I remember Dolly as a kind, compassionate caring person who was another of those much-loved Ketley characters. 'Lolly Dolly', as the children affectionately called her, passed on a few years ago but her memory lives on in the form of a plaque on the front facing wall of the Ketley school.

The plaque provided by a grateful authority was dedicated by local councillor Pauline Picken reads as follows; 'In memory of Dolly Amoss our

School Crossing Warden who devoted twenty-seven years to the safety of the children of Ketley. Unveiled on behalf of the people of Ketley parish by Mrs. Pauline Picken 31st of January 1993'.

Falsely regarded as another 'Ketley Mon', John Lees was in fact born locally but not in Ketley. John was born near the border of Ketley in nearby Hadley but his story is interwoven into rich tapestry of the modern day history of Ketley.

People that know John today may find it difficult to believe that his first tenuous steps in business consisted of combing the Ketley council tip for rags! From those difficult and ground floor beginnings he gradually inched his way to the position of a well-respected self-made businessman. In 1975 he found himself back in Ketley via his modest 'Glory Hole' shop in the St. George's High Street.

The turning point came with the Conversion of the Second World War munitions factory of William Henry Lane fame into a furniture and carpet warehouse. Little did John know that the name that would be synonymous with that building to this day!

He recalls that on the opening day a solitary bedroom suite was the only item on display but, within an hour, he had sold it and set the pattern for the future.

The former 'tip rat' eventually gained a more creditable nickname as 'The Dealer'. From the premises known as the 'Glory Hole' John brought affordable items of furniture and household goods to thousands of eager customers. Ordinary working class people benefited from 'good deals' and John became a very popular and well-known figure in and around the midlands.

Locally he is well known for his passionate patriotism and his generosity towards local charities, but the ex-soldier still retains his dealer's instinct and his 'eye' for a bargain.

Eventually, almost inevitively, Lees spread his new empire to foreign fields. He hit on the original idea of buying up old red PO telephones and exporting them to the culture starved Americans, and Ex-patriot Brits, to use as converted shower cubicles or symbols of home. It amused him when travellers along the old A5 would pull up at the sight of a row of telephone boxes at the Glory Hole.

He got a kick out of watching 'punters' attempt to make phone calls from his shower/telephones. He lost count of the times someone would complain that they couldn't get a line out!

The tinker who went from door to door peddler-like buying and selling second hand furniture and nick-knack's is another self-made millionaire.

John is proud of his achievements in life and in common with other self-made people of the area has never abandoned his working-class roots. He knows what it's like to be poor; he has lived on the street and foraged for 'tat' on waste tips.

A PERSONAL VIEW

"Thee knowst what they say about a Ketley mon dustner? A Ketley mon never gets beat, he either wins or meks a draw."

Words in the old Ketley slang that form in my head today easily as they did fifty years ago. I have carried them with me for all that time. When I was a boy most of my fellow Ketley residents spoke the old language. Considered low caste and a sign of a lack of sophistication then, it is rightly regarded today as an important part of our precious heritage. You may regard it as silly that a grown man would put such store by a corny phrase but, as a proud 'Ketley mon', I swear there were times those words gave me the resolve to face whatever problem I came across, especially during my working life.

I first heard the phrase when I was an impressionable six or seven years of age. Len Corbett the third eldest of four brothers that lived next door was and still is one of the proudest Ketley men I ever met. Lenny, as he was known, and his brothers Graham, Alan and Roy together with a hand full of others still use the old slang. They are probably considered old fashioned by most but their stance on moral issues, sense of fair play and a healthy respect for all things natural made them 'eco warriors' long before the phrase was invented.

Lenny, who is THE Ketley character in his own right, was more popularly known by the nickname of 'the Ketley Paddy'. There were two basic reasons for this name, his love of a pint of Guinness (or to be honest, his love for several pints of 'dark stuff'), and a lifetime spent in the tarmac and construction gangs dominated by Irishmen, generally known in the pre-politically correct days as 'Paddys'.

Ketley Main road, also known as the A5, looking westerly towards Wellington in the early 1950s.
(Picture loaned by Ray Pritchard)

Lenny is one of the few surviving links between the legendary Ketley characters, Billy Foulkes and Jack Spragg and modern-day Ketley. When I visited his Wellington flat this hard-edged, stoutly built 'Ketley Mon' showed a rare glimpse of emotion. With a hint of a tear in his eye Lenny waxed lyrical at the mere mention of his old pals, revealing a side to his character that I had never witnessed before.

The thought ran through my mind, 'would this died-in-the-wool Ketley Mon consider his show of emotion as a 'win, draw, or loss'?

Research for this book has brought me into contact with many of the surviving 'old' Ketley people, awakening long forgotten memories and experiences from my early days. I was born in the back bedroom of 5 Victoria Avenue, Ketley on Sunday 21st March 1943, and a day that is traditionally celebrated as the first day of spring. My mother used to tell me that I was special because I was firstborn and 'came in with the spring', which was a special time of the year.

In common with most babies of that time I was delivered by the local district nurse, Emmie Hendrie who hailed from Red Lake. Her proud boast was that she had smacked the arse of every Ketley kid even before the masters at Ketley School!

Christened at the Ketley Parish Church in Red Lake I was named Leonard (after my dad and my grandmothers favourite brother who had been killed in the First World War), William after my maternal grandfather, and Terence after a cousin in Shrewsbury, but I have always been referred to as Terry.

Emma and Bert Lowe, my grandparents had moved to number five from the slum standard houses known as the Ketley Offices when they were demolished under the redevelopment scheme in 1935.

This period also saw the provision of new housing at the Broadway Estate on the Hadley road, Castle View, Red Lake and Sinclair Gardens, Ketley Town.

In 1939 work had begun on the new Overdale Estate but when war was declared, the half finished buildings were left until the end of hostilities and finally completed ten years after the foundations were laid.

A dozen or so former Ketley Offices residents were re-housed in the Victoria Avenue area and were not sorry to see the end of appalling conditions. Earth toilets, community wash house and polluted water from the 'spike', a local spring source, were swapped for gas lighting and an indoor flush toilet and the extreme luxury of a hot bath.

In many cases the housing authorities placed families next to their previous neighbours, partly explaining the unusually strong community spirit of the new Avenue residents.

A few families remained over at the Ketley Offices and the Saturday night exodus included boys like Allan Parton coming over to take his

Ketley Hall as seen in this 1999 view. At the end of a school day I would sometimes play in the spacious grounds of Ketley Hall that my schoolmate Michael Smith lived in. Ketley Hall was also known as Ketley Hill Hall and was in complete contrast to my overcrowded semi-detached council house in Victoria Avenue. *(Terry Lowe)*

weekly bath at his Aunt Ada Thompson's new house, which was next door to our family in Victoria Avenue.

Many of the families were inter-related, inevitable in a tightly knit community like Ketley. I like the wit in the story of Margaret Chappel's first venture into local politics. Having failed to get elected, Ada, Margaret's mother asked how many votes her daughter had polled and when Margaret replied, "230" Ada retorted, "230? Theest got more relatives than that"!

As another example I only recently discovered that our next door neighbours, the Corbett boys were our second cousins, our respective grandmothers had been sisters. This fact might go a long way to explaining my affinity with Lenny and perhaps another reason for my first name?

Another point, which may seem remarkable today, is that most of the thirty semi-detached houses of Victoria Avenue were home to two, and sometimes three families. At one stage six adults and five younsters lived in our three-bedroom home.

I was the first born, followed by my cousin Alan. My brother Ken was next swiftly followed by cousin Christine. My Aunt Florrie and Uncle Bill moved with their children Alan and Christine to the new estate at Mannerley Lane in 1949. When their third child, Brian was due my grandmother, who was the matriarch of the family insisted that her daughter return 'home' to have the latest edition to the clan born under her watchful eye. My youngest brother, Barry, completed the total of kids born in number five.

The Avenue was the epicentre of my early life. My oldest memory is of my Uncle Bill Parton, Florrie's husband, returning home from the war in his khaki battledress.

I also remember a pig in a sty at the bottom of our garden and gathering fresh eggs from the dozens of chickens and bantam hens that roamed the small garden. Everything was geared to self-sufficiency. There were no supermarkets or garden centres in those days, we grew or reared practically everything we ate and nothing was wasted, scraps and swill were re-cycled through the pigs and eggshells ground up and re-fed to the fowl providing vitally needed grit.

I read of a survey recently that claimed most people today don't even know the name of their next door neighbours let alone have any social contact with them.

That's a far cry from the halcyon days of post war Ketley when every body seemed to know everybody else and, as residents, used to wander unhindered into any of the other houses in the Avenue.

Unlocked doors proved the absence of the so-called 'fear of crime'. The community spirit was nowhere stronger than in the close-knit Victoria Avenue. The residents were, after all, probably related!

Thinking back now I realised that at one time or another I have seen inside every one of the thirty homes in the Avenue, which strikes me as a remarkable statement to make in the light of the recent survey.

Ada Thompson, next door to us at number four, had been the driving force behind 'Ketley Shamrocks Jazz Band'. Formed during the war it was dominated by people from our street, including leader, Margaret and her brother Alf.

Alf had told me how my parents and many other local courting couples found the band an ideal opportunity to carry out their courting. The local Horseshoes pub's backfield was a perfect place to practice their routines, and, of course a handy place to quench their thirst when they finished. Everybody was encouraged to take part even children. In a picture taken at a local carnival my next door neighbour Graham Corbett, brother Lenny and mate Billy Hall looked smart in their drummer boy uniforms. Billy Hall would have been the nephew of the drowned Bunty Hall; he was, in fact, named after his late uncle. Billy's proud claim is that he was the first child born in Victoria Avenue.

The residents began their move to the Avenue in October 1934, four months before Billy was born. He is another of those die-hard Ketley men who have only moved a matter of yards from where they were born. Graham Corbett was dubbed locally as the 'worlds oldest paper boy', a nickname gained from his first little job. From the age of about thirteen to well into adult hood Graham could be seen hurtling around the Ketley area on local shopkeeper Alf Whittinghams black trade bike, delivering the news and groceries.

Graham is the equivalent of a walking, talking local directory. He can still name every family, road name, house number and grocery and newspaper choice of 1950s Ketley.

Today the shop that was the mainstay of our local needs is known as Crusty Ken's, selling fresh sandwiches, continuing a tenuous link to the grocery trade.

Graham retained his thick local accent but the old black bike has been replaced by an immaculately preserved old Austin Traveller estate car. His accent is so thick and delivered at a machine-gun pace even I have difficulty keeping up with him!

He still lives in the heart of Ketley at the Incline, spending his time looking after his goats and 'chewing the fat' with his mates in one of the local pubs. Apart from the compulsory military service, Graham, in common with most of his generation, has spent his entire life in Ketley.

The Avenue is horseshoe shaped and in those days was surrounded by fields, which, to me, gave the place the pleasant feeling of being a kind of safe haven.

On the Avenues backfield I learnt my football and that most important lesson in life, how to take a bloody nose as well as give one.

If anybody in the street had a problem, say with a motor bike or car, my dad or Percy Wood from number twenty-six would help fix it and Bernard

Lenny Corbett, the original Ketley Mon with a conger eel. The picture is taken outside the Wren's Nest public house where the sea-fishing club was based.
(Picture loaned by Lenny Corbett)

Steventon from twenty-four was our very own medic. Employed at the Ketley works as an ambulance-man in the works clinic, he doubled up as the firms football team medic. As a St. John's Ambulance Officer he was unofficially 'on call for twenty-four hours' in the Avenue for a myriad of ailments and minor accidents.

Bernard was a genuinely nice man, quietly spoken, unflappable and deeply religious. He was an accomplished lay preacher at the Central Methodist Church in Ketley, and was another of those persons that everybody loved and respected.

I'm a little surprised today at how parochial we were then, best illustrated on the sports field. Football was our staple sport and local fixtures against Ketley Town, Overdale or the Brook would be fierce affairs and 'away' games in neighbouring Hadely resembled a war zone always ending with tears before bed for the losers, (usually Hadley). Ketley has a proud tradition of football.

In 1895 the 'Ketley Victorians' was the local team. Consisting entirely of Ketley miners and ironworkers the team successfully competed in an area league with other local workers teams.

Sixty years later two local boys became the latest Ketley lads to play professional soccer. Anthony Harris, nicknamed, 'Razzer' had been an amateur with the Red Lake based St. Mary's Youth Club since he was twelve.

Derick Dawes who hailed from the Ketley borderline area known as 'The Rock' had been outstanding for the nearby Dawley eleven. Both boys graduated to the status of professional footballer. In 1962 they joined the Counties only league side, Shrewsbury Town. That year Shrewsbury's colts, a team contained no less than five Shropshire born players.

Looking west along the A5 at Ketley cross roads in a view taken around 1950. The Wesleyan Chapel can be seen in the centre of the picture. The chapel was also known as the Central Methodist Church, the name used for the new building.
(Picture loaned by Ray Pritchard)

Razzer and Derick played with distinction in the Shrews first team and became firm favourite with local fans. Derrick was a particularly gifted as a footballer.

He possessed an array of silky skills and what is referred to as a 'footballers brain'.

Razzer was transferred to Bradford in the late 1960s and later immigrated to Australia and Derick transferred to local amateur rivals Wellington Town to enable him to take a job and continue with the sport he loved.

Another talented young Ketley boy who was born at number seven in the Avenue played semi-professional football for a season at Telford United (formally Wellington Town). The twenty-year-old grandson of 'Jacker' Rigby, Gwyn Parry was a prolific centre forward and played amateur football till he was well into his forties.

Then there was 'the one that got away'! Dennis Spragg from Victoria Avenue played in goal for Billy Upton's Ketley Boys Brigade during the Second World War, graduating to keeper of the net at the then, prestigious Allied Ironworks eleven. Following a string of impressive performances between the sticks, 'Tedlar' Parton, Alan's dad, who was a scout for fist division Huddersfield, persuaded them to come to Shropshire to see the boy play. Dennis got wind of the arrangement and failed to turn up. Another Victoria Avenue boy, Johnny Williams substituted for the fifteen year old Dennis who, bizarrely watched the game from a distance not having the nerve to show himself. Dennis has always regretted letting Tedlar down.

A fiercely proud Tedlar never spoke to Dennis from that cold 1940s Saturday morning to the day he died many years later.

Ketley School boasted a football team. Shown here are the early 1940s players. Rear row includes Bob Edge, Billy Tonks, Trevor Williams, Ken Thomas, Albert Pritchard. On the middle row are Wesley Weston, Albert Hendy, Bob Diss, John Bedall, Frank Newnes, while on the bottom row are Eddie Lane, Peter Rigby and Fred Parton. *(loaned by Trevor Williams)*

Dedication ceremony of the new Red Lake cemetery in 1954. Those attending were Ray Hutchinson, Len Bevan, Teddy Freeman, Eric Purcell on the back row and Emmie Hendrie, Phillips, Billy Upton and Andrew Hasden in front. *(Wellington Journal and Shrewsbury News - courtesy Shropshire Star)*

Ketley Carrnival Queen in 1958. Behind Pam Jenkins who was elected Queen that year are Bill Yates MP, Russ Hamilton, Reverend Davies and Benny Foster. Attendents were Mary Huxley, the Foster children and Jill Bowen. *(Wellington Journal and Shrewsbury News - courtesy Shropshire Star)*

The majority of the Victoria Avenue residents epitomised the working classes of the time, and most of them were larger than life characters in their own right.

The pre-television days allowed for a social calendar of sport and community generated entertainment, usually linked to the local public house. Margaret Thompson the baton carrier and leader of the local Jazz band rallied the residents to make their own entertainment and have fun and adventure at the same time. She was an inspirational and natural born leader.

As a single-minded dedicated local champion she went on to make her own mark in politics as a hard-working local councillor, rising to the heady heights of Chair of the Wrekin District Council in the 1970s.

As Margaret Chappell she and her Yorkshire born husband Tom, who was also an elected councillor slaved tirelessly for the benefit of her home town area carrying on the work begun in the 1930s by the likes of Upton, Wormstone, Hutchinson, and others.

Three doors away from Margaret's home lived what was probably the largest family unit in the Avenue. Jacker and Jinny Rigby's brood of six daughters and one son and their various partners all shared the terraced house's three bedrooms. The youngest daughter Hilda was, and still is a Ketley beauty. Witty and intelligent, she grew up to be another fiercely partisan politician and following in her near neighbour's footsteps she picked up where Margaret left off fighting for 'Ketley's cause. As Hilda Rhodes she also held the Office of Chair of the old Wrekin District Council in the 1990s. This former Sunday School teacher's ever-smiling appearance belies her political sharpness and dedication. Hilda Rhodes still serves her local area as councillor and as another passionate Ketley champion she ensures that the area is not overlooked or short-changed. Hilda is one of only a handful of people that have survived from the original Avenue settlers to still live in the street. Hilda and husband Bernard occupy number 28 while Charlie and Elsie Purcell, who live next door at 29, have the single distinction of still living in their original home in an unbroken tenure lasting over sixty years! Hilda's brother Ronnie also shares a near lifetime in the Avenue at the Rigby family home, number seven.

At the other end of the scale less than half a mile away Ketley's grandest dwelling provided a stark contrast to the local council houses.

Approximately 200 yards south of the schools buildings stands one of the counties most imposing and important buildings, Ketley Hall.

At the end of a school day I would sometimes play in the spacious grounds of the house that my schoolmate Michael Smith lived in. Ketley Hall, which was also known as Ketley Hill Hall was in complete contrast to my overcrowded semi-detached council house in Victoria Avenue. It is uncertain when it was built but the Audley family sold it to James Leveson-Gower in 1528.

The most famous residents were the Reynolds and Williams families of the golden age of iron and coal followed by a Wellington printer called Jams Keay.

In 1938 Cyril and Josephine Smith acquired the Hall and the family remain in situ today. As a small boy I had no idea of the importance of the great house where I played Cowboys and Indians among the buildings and plantations.

The 1950s proved to be a decade of significant change for the inhabitants of Ketley with the 1960s heralding what many believed to be the beginning of Ketley's decline. It was also a time of great change for me. In the ten years from 1950 to 1960 I had grown from boy to man. I had experienced historic events such as the passing of a King and the crowning of a Queen, outer-space exploration and the advent of television. I had also changed schools and graduated to the status of 'working man'.

In June 1953 when our present Queen was crowned the children of the Avenue were treated to a party at the Central Methodist Chapel. The majority of my fellow Avenue dwellers were Sunday School pupils at the Chapel, as I was.

Linda Mary Socket, my form teacher at Ketley School, took full advantage of the occasion by having us compile scrapbooks with material and pictures on the 'New Elizabethans' theme.

In the same year I saw, like thousands of others, my first television set.

The coronation of the new Queen sent thousands to electrical dealers to purchase television sets. Frank Swift of Red Lake, who had previously provided most of the radios in the Ketley area, was now busy installing the invention of the age.

A Group of Ketley children outside Ketley Central Methodist Church on Coronation Day in June 1953. All bar one of the children in the picture were residents of Victoria Avenue.
(Terry Lowe)

My step-uncle, Eric Barnett was the first in our family to have a set and invited us all down to his home in Hadley to see the Cup Final. To be honest the flickering grey images of Stanley Matthew's swerving his way to his medal didn't impress me.

As a regular cinemagoer I was hooked on the big screen and my early heroes, Roy Rogers and Humphrey Bogart!

If I could pick one memory to relive from those times it would be a Lowe family annual holiday which took place each year at the same time, the last week in July and first week in August with the close-down of Sankey's factory where dad and granddad worked. In the weeks leading up to the trip my brother, cousins and I saved every penny, constantly checking and counting the coins up to the moment of departure. The excitement of the event ensured a sleepless Friday night. We always left in convoy at 9.am on the Saturday morning for the eighty mile trek to the Welsh seaside resort of Rhyl. Three cars, six adults and nine children made their way to number 44 Abbey Street, Rhyl for a week of sea, sand and 'kiss me quick hats'.

Prior to the 1950s the group now known as 'teenagers' were non-existent, but two movie films changed all that.

'Blackboard Jungle', an X rated tale of American youngsters in a tough Bronx school spawned Rock and Roll music and rebellious 'teenagers'. James Dean in 'Rebel Without a Cause' gave us the icon to model our newfound status on.

In 1957 the St Mary's Church held a Summer Fete on Bailey's field at Red Lake. British Cycle team manager Benny Foster pulled off a coupe when he persuaded Singer/actor Frankie Vaughan to open the Fete.

The Liverpool born Vaughan who was appearing at the Granada Theatre in Shrewsbury at the time was the nearest we would get to Hollywood. The event opened in glorious June sunshine with Ann Hardy (sister of Bob and Tony) from Overdale being crowned as Queen by Frankie. The event was a huge success with the Sankey's Castle Works band providing live music.

There were numerous stalls and sporting events including a clock golf competition run by the local headmaster, Mr Dodd. Reading the sad news of Frankie Vaughan's death in 1999 brought back the happy memories of when a star came to Ketley on a sunny summer's day.

In 1958 the St Mary's Fete committee decided to continue the 'pop' theme by bringing in a one hit wonder singer called Russ Hamilton to crown local girl Pam Jenkins as Queen. This event was another well-organised success but with the advent of televisions invading more and more homes and the popularity of the new rock music bringing live concerts to the fore, carnivals and fetes were virtually doomed.

In 1958 I witnessed the another piece of 'old Ketley' vanish under the bulldozers wheels with the demolition of the old Forge Row and famous 'Mission Building'.

Seven Stars public house and crossroads as seen from the pit mound behind Whittinham's' fish and chip shop. *(Picture loaned by Ray Pritchard)*

In its place came the construction of the Sandbrook Estate and ironically I ended up living on the site of the old Forge Row. On Friday July 11th 1958 I left school and on the following Monday, the 14th my salad days ended when I began a maintenance fitters apprenticeship at the Joseph Sankey and Sons works at Hadley. I was fifteen years and three months old. One year later my parents finally moved into their own home at 7 Sandbrook after sixteen years of married life.

In 1962 Dawley New Town became the 18th town to be designated since the passing of the New Towns Act of 1946. The initial plan was for just over 9,000 acres from within the urban districts of Dawley, Madeley Ward, the Borough of Wenlock, Ironbridge and Coalbrookdale, parts of Oakengates and Shifnal parishes and the Wellington rural District which included Ketley to comprise the new Town. From that moment slowly but surely the whole area including Ketley took on a new appearance.

I'm not one of those that yearn for the 'good old days' because I believe they were far from being the good old days. We tend to think of the past with fondness because we usually only recall the good things that we experienced. I would have hated the polluted water, earth toilets, twelve-hour working days and poor working conditions that my ancestors had to endure.

Progress by definition should bring improvement and in my opinion in the case of the new town of Telford that has in general terms been achieved but at the cost of losing the identities of many of the small towns which existed before Telford. Ketley was one of those towns. Familiar landmarks disappeared under the planner's timetable. A major blow came three days before Christmas Day in 1964 the oldest coaching inn on the old A5 fell to the demolition team. Pictured here are *(above)* the demolition of the Queens Head in September 1973 and *(below)* the Seven Stars in December 1964. *(Pictures courtesy Shopshire Star)*

Progress by definition should bring improvement and in my opinion in the case of the new town of Telford that has in general terms been achieved but at the cost of losing the identities of many of the small towns which existed before Telford. Ketley was one of those towns. Familiar landmarks disappeared under the planner's timetable. A major blow came three days before Christmas Day in 1962 the oldest coaching inn on the old A5 fell to the demolition team.

The popular Elizabethan pub known as the Seven Stars complete with it's own resident ghost brought a tear to many a local drinkers eye, including yours truly, when it finally lay in a pile of 16th Century rubble. I used to patronise the old pub, which was drenched in character. The sloping floor and the Elizabethan beams which were so low-slung regulars used to bet on how many unsuspecting punters banged their heads on them, and that was before they had taken a drink!

The reason, they say, for this act of what many believe was pure vandalism was the straightening the old staggered crossroads.

A new Seven Stars was built in a site further back from the roadside which has been modernised and turned into what is called a 'fun pub' today. Now called the Elephant and Castle there is nothing to mark the historical significance of the old site. The new pub was bigger and brasher but was bereft of any character.

Earlier in the year another sad event occurred in Ketley when the last passenger train steamed out of the local station on the evening of Saturday 21th July 1962. A small group of enthusiasts gathered on the little station platform to witness the historic event. The train from Much Wenlock disappeared within it's own smoke as it headed for Wellington. The Ketley Junction Box situated near to the rail spur off the Wellington to Wolverhampton tracks was removed together with the track back up to the Ketley Town Junction. During the next two years supply trains continued to feed the Ketley Works from the Madeley Junction through Lightmore and on to Ketley Town. In 1964 the line closed altogether. Railway historian and author Ken Jones had told me of the 'Hop Pickers Special' that operated during the 1930s. George Weston of Ketley Brook organised Ketley pickers for the special train that carried them through to Tenbury Wells to help with the hop picking.

Complete families were known to take advantage of earning extra cash and having a holiday at the same time in the hugely popular scheme. The last stationmaster to live in the Ketley Station House was a chap called Ted Davies who retired in 1933 at the height of the railways' popularity.

The honour of being the last Ketley stationmaster fell to a Mr Rumble who lived at Horsehay. The final occupants of the Ketley Station House were a family named Pearson. Bill Pearson was a relief signalman and lived at the house by virtue of the fact that he was an employee of the Railway Company.

During the 1930s the latest incumbent of Ketley Hall, Wellington Printer James Keay, had provided a beautifully bound Bible for the spiritual comfort of the travellers. He had it placed in the station's tiny waiting room.

No one knows today what happened to the Bible but an unnamed Hadley source sarcastically commented " It was probably not well thumbed because half the buggers from Ketley conner read and the other half dunner go to church".

The old railway line is unrecognisable today having become an overgrown litter-strewn pathway to Sinclair Gardens and Parkers pool – a favourite with dog owners. The only reminder of its past is a faint trace of white paint on the little piece of platform that remains.

In moments of nostalgia I stand still on what's left of the old platform and I swear I can smell the distinctive smokestack and hear the chuff-chuff of the Ketley Dodger as it clanks its way along the single track line to Saturday Market at Wellington!

Other familiar landmarks of the area began slowly disappearing during the 1950s and 1960s. The Central Methodist Chapel, Florrie Bagnal's Cafe and shop and the adjoining housing was demolished to be replaced with the Seven Hills and Reynolds House flats. The new Methodist Church adjacent to the flats is a fitting replacement for the old chapel. I have happy memories of the old Victorian building known as the Central Chapel.

The last train left Ketley in 1962. Shown here is the station platform and siding where a goods truck has come to rest. During the next two years supply trains continued to feed the Ketley Works from the Madeley Junction through Lightmore and on to Ketley Town.
(Picture loaned by John Whittingham)

It was there in its Sunday School that I and my fellow devotees pledged ourselves as 'sunbeams for Jesus'. Generations of local children, including me, dressed in their Sunday best boarded the annual Anniversary stage. We would perform on a specially built platform in rows, with freshly scrubbed faces, to the delight of our proud parents.

The autumn of 1964 brought much needed commerce and jobs to the town in the shape of the counties award-winning newspaper, the Shropshire Star.

The mountain of pennestone clay disappeared to make way for the paper's offices and presses. A 'Small Business' park occupies the area South of the Star offices, previously known, locally as 'the plantation'; the area was rich in wildlife and fauna.

In 1971, ninety-one-year old Jimmy Wormstone and eighty-one- year old Billy Upton were guests of honour at the official opening of the Ketley Recreational Centre by J D Craddock, Chairman of the Wellington rural District Council.

Situated at the Ketley playing field the centre included a sports building and an open-air swimming pool. An old pit mound on the specially designed grounds remains today as a tribute to the towns past glories.

Ageing former councillors, still politically astute, reminded the 300 plus guests that this was the culmination of the work they had started thirty-seven years previously.

The hard fought for playing field gates were moved from their roadside location to a more peaceful part of the re-designed fields. The customary swings, slide and climbing frames were enhanced with a dirt track for bikes and a five a side football pitch.

Still echoing to the happy sounds of children at play, Reverend Samuel Cadman, who dedicated the gates nearly forty years previously, would be pleased. The garden area is a tranquil place in which to spend a sunny afternoon. An abundance of songbirds and flora and fauna add to the ambience.

Ketley councillor Ray Hutchinson, chairman of the council's playing fields and parks committee informed the crowd that since the swimming pool had opened five weeks previously 6,000 people had used the facility.

The project was completed two years later when a golf driving range and squash court complex was added. The Recreational Centre re-named as The Parkside Centre is still in use for local groups as a meeting place, and home for the Ketley Good Companion's Club.

Located in what is probable the true centre of the old town it is the closest we have got to a Town Hall. The old campaigners would approve.

Unfortunately the swimming pool ceased trading some years ago and was raised to the ground in the spring of 1999.

In the early 1970s the pool was the scene of a double drowning. Two young men had climbed the pools outer wall to take a midnight swim following a night out, but unfortunately they got into trouble and perished in the cold waters of the night.

The Telford and Wrekin Council run Ketley Leisure Golf Squash and Fitness Centre is now also closed and on the doomed list; victim of new plans to build a new road that will pass through part of the playing fields.

The 1970s proved to be a time of major change for Ketley with the first stretch of the M54 motorway opening in 1975 sealing the fate of yet another Ketley landmark in the shape of the locally famous murder pub the Queens Head. The scene of Jane Edges' demise was reduced to another pile of rubble to make way for the new motorway slip road and a traffic island, appropriately named, 'Ketley Brook Island' providing a silent reminder of happier days when Ketley Brook was a bustling community.

A year later the Ketley Civil Parish Council was formed from the former Wellington Rural Parish which in turn had been formed in 1880.

Memories of the old Ketley carnival days were briefly stirred in 1977 when a fun day and comic football match was held on the playing field to celebrate the Queens Silver Jubilee, sadly the days of dozens of jazz bands, fancy dress and carnival floats had disappeared, perhaps for ever. Another brief glimpse of those days came in 1988 at the 'Ketley Fiesta'. Celebrating the 150th birthday of the Ketley Parish Church.

A small flotilla of vehicles and revellers followed a route through Red Lake. Overdale and Ketley Town back up to Potters Bank and the carnival field at Red Lake. Someone came up with the highly original idea of having television weather man John Kettley open the event.

Reverting briefly to ancient tradition, field events, a couple of jazz bands and dancing troupes brought back happy memories to the older folk present. Sadly this was one of the last mass community gatherings in the town of Ketley.

When housing developers threatened the existence of the eleven-acre site known as Paddock Mound they underestimated the resolve and fighting spirit of the locals.

For historical and ecological reasons this little piece of Ketley had to be defended.

Generations of Ketley schoolchildren had experienced nature at first hand in the pools and grounds of the Paddock and the remains of Reynolds 18th Century canal were part of Ketley's heritage. In a show of what is called 'people power' today a small group of preservationists including resident locals, Fen Tiler, Mike and Sue Wilkinson and Angela Shepherd to their eternal credit decided to fight the proposal.

In a campaign designed to rally the locals they fought a long drawn-out battle to final victory.

Mr P M Keyte succeeded as headmaster in 1948 and is remembered for the ground breaking idea of adopting a ship. Through the British Ship Adoption Society 'SS Tydeus', owned by Thomas Holte of the famous Blue Funnel Line was chosen by the Ketley school children. Shown in this picture are Jimmy Wormstone, Trevor Williams, Captain Renshaw, Headmaster Keyte and student Diane Oakes on the right. Hazel Merrington, on the left is next to Mrs Renshaw. *(Picture loaned by Trevor Williams)*

Councillor Hilda Rhodes, in her capacity as Chair of the Wrekin District Council supported and attended a ceremony to mark the completion of the land reclamation scheme at the Paddock Mound where she unveiled a plaque on a 'kissing gate' donated by the 'Paddock Mound Conservation Group'. The council had co-ordinated the project which included making safe three mineshafts, landscaping, fencing and footpaths. The old canal bed was dredged and the pond was restored ensuring that future generations can enjoy the wildlife and flora and fauna of the area.

As a realist but eternal optimist, I'm convinced that my hometown will exist long after most of us have passed on, if in name only. The mines have long gone and the Furnace is on a life support, but the commerce is strong.

The world famous Aga Rayburn cooker ranges has its roots in Ketley, the Shropshire Star newspaper has won national awards for journalism, add to them two major car dealerships in the shape of Vauxhall and Peugeot brings trade to the area.

The motorway, which was supposed to bring much needed relief to the main road of Ketley, has had an opposite effect. The former A5 is today busier than ever, unfortunately most travellers are just passing through.

Ketley, as seen in 1999. This picture is the up-to-date view of that shown on the cover which was taken from the same place during the demolition of Ketley Offices in a view supplied courtesy of the Shropshire Star. *(Terry Lowe)*

The Ketley skyline has changed drastically. Forge Row, Ketley Offices and Days Buildings replaced by Sandbrook and a petrol station and tyre depot. Gone forever the score of shops and pubs that once dotted the main road. Names that were common fifty years ago, Dunnings Store, Beards Butchers, Alf Whittinghams grocers, Ernie Clements cycle shop and Archie Greens post office are all history.

The only time you will hear of them is when two or more older Ketley folk are gathered together, probably over a pint!

As I approach the final few words of my view on Ketley I have to say that this work is by no means the definitive Ketley story.

The intention was to do what has never been done and that was to write a book about my town, and I believe I have done that. I'm sure critics will say this or that has been omitted or this or that should not have been included, my answer to that is, to paraphrase the famous American President Abraham Lincoln, when he said, "You can't please all of the people all of the time".

I now have a fresh optimism. In one way or another Ketley will survive, if only in the memories of its people and my words.

Through the efforts of the preservationists part of the old canal route can be traced and every hill and mound that survive within Ketley's borders reminds us of its glorious contribution to the past. Unfortunately the environment still suffers.

The latest batch of houses have cut a swathe though the gorse and hedgerows of Cow Wood where a previously unsolved murder took place and Lilly Boardman fed almost tame local foxes! The cost of this development is in the dwindling wildlife and plant life and hammering what some believe is another nail in the Ketley coffin. Whatever the future may bring I pray that my beloved Ketley will survive.

One final plea; if you find yourself passing through Ketley on the great and ancient Roman Road do yourself a favour stop and visit what I believe is one of the rightful centres of the world famous Industrial Revolution, before its too late.

Selwyn Walker provided the coach and trimmings for the carnival queen.

ISBN 1 897990 99 5

Type-set and distributed by British Bus Publishing Ltd
16 St Margaret's Drive, Wellington, Telford, TF1 3PH
Telephone: 01952 255669 - Facsimile: 01952 222397 - E-mail: billpotter@britishbuspublishing.co.uk